M·E·N·U · M·A·S·T·E·R·S

CHINESE COOKERY

EDITED BY
JENNI TAYLOR

OCTOPUS BOOKS

MENU-MATCH CODE

To allow more flexibility within the menus we have added
bold numbers after certain recipes to offer suitable
alternatives.
Thus, if the numbers ·3·11·14· appear after a starter, they
indicate that the starter of Menu 3, 11, or 14 could be
substituted.
Using the MENU-MATCH CODE you will be sure to find
a menu to suit all tastes.

NOTES

Standard spoon measurements are used in all recipes
1 tablespoon – one 15 ml spoon
1 teaspoon – one 5 ml spoon
All spoon measures are level
Where amounts of salt and pepper are not specified, the
cook should use his/her own discretion.
Canned foods should not be drained, unless so stated in the
recipe. For all recipes, quantities are given in metric and
imperial measures. Follow one set of measures only,
because they are not interchangeable.

Jacket photography: Pork with mushrooms and bean
sprouts; Prawns in tomato sauce; Honeyed pears.

First published 1986 by
Octopus Books Limited
59 Grosvenor Street, London W 1
© 1986 Octopus Books Limited
ISBN 0 7064 2679 7

Produced by Mandarin Publishers Ltd
22a Westlands Rd
Quarry Bay, Hong Kong
Printed in Hong Kong

C · O · N · T · E · N · T · S

I·N·T·R·O·D·U·C·T·I·O·N

The key to Chinese cookery is presentation and harmony. This isn't difficult to achieve, provided you plan ahead. In this book, we've done the planning for you. Follow our menus and you'll see how the balance is achieved. Each meal is designed to illustrate how different ingredients can be combined and how contrasting cooking methods can be used effectively.

Costly? No. The Chinese recognize that you can have too much of a good thing. Expensive ingredients are used in small quantities, usually finely chopped so that their flavours are distributed throughout a dish, but set against the backdrop of staples like rice, noodles and vegetables.

As you gain in confidence you'll soon be planning your own Chinese meals. Remember that at informal family gatherings all the dishes are served at once, simply placed in the middle of the table. Each guest has a bowl for soup, another for rice, a spoon and chopsticks, and helps himself.

Formal entertaining is more elaborate, with several courses and wines. Opt for Chinese rice wine or a light fruity white or red grape wine. Start by serving one or two hors d'oeuvres, which should be on the table when your guests arrive. To follow, two or three stir-fried dishes and maybe a soup. The special dish of the meal, perhaps Peking Duck or Chinese Hot Pot, should then be presented. Or you could serve a selection of steamed or braised dishes with plain or fried rice. Elaborate desserts seldom feature in Chinese cuisine; instead tea traditionally concludes the meal.

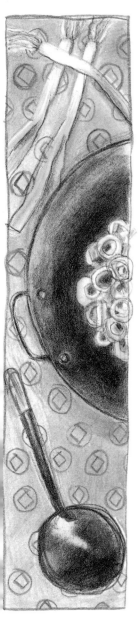

M·E·N·U

· 1 ·

Family Supper for 4

Lemon Chicken or
Fish and Bean Curd Casserole
Hot-tossed Vegetables
Meat Cubes in Bean Sauce
Plain Boiled Rice (page 12)

This casual menu is typical of Chinese fare as it contains a little of each of the three 'meats' – fish, meat and poultry – and the lightly cooked, crisp vegetable dish without which no family meal is complete. It is served with plain boiled rice, fried rice being reserved for more formal occasions. It is traditional to serve all dishes simultaneously at a family meal and since the time-consuming aspect of cooking Chinese food is the preparation it is essential that you set aside plenty of time for chopping and slicing the raw ingredients. Being well prepared will enable you to enjoy a hassle-free meal even if you have to produce several stir-fry dishes at the last minute.

Chinese Soups

A soup may be served as an accompaniment to the meal and may be enjoyed at any stage, along with the other dishes. For this reason, most Chinese soups are clear stocks to which small pieces of meat and vegetables are added just before serving. On more formal occasions, a soup may appear between each course to act as a neutralizer, cleansing the palate. It can even be served at the end of a meal. To make a clear stock follow the recipe on page 31 and add to the ingredients of your choice. Tea is usually served at the end of the meal rather than as a beverage accompanying it. It is seldom served with the food.

Lemon Chicken

Metric/Imperial

1 × 1.5-2 kg/3-4 lb chicken, boned and cut into bite-size
   pieces
1½ teaspoons salt
freshly ground black pepper
5 tablespoons oil
15 g/½ oz lard
4 slices root ginger, peeled and chopped
1 red pepper, cored, seeded and shredded
5-6 Chinese dried mushrooms, soaked in warm water for
   20 minutes, squeezed dry, stemmed and shredded
grated rind of 2 lemons
5 spring onions, thinly sliced
4 tablespoons rice wine or dry sherry
1½ teaspoons sugar
2 tablespoons light soy sauce
1 teaspoon cornflour, dissolved in 1 tablespoon water
1-2 tablespoons lemon juice

1. Rub the chicken all over with the salt, pepper and 1½ tablespoons of the oil. Heat the remaining oil in a wok over high heat. Add the chicken and stir-fry for 2 minutes then remove, drain and keep warm.
2. Add the lard to the pan. When the fat has melted, add the root ginger, red pepper and mushrooms. Stir-fry for 1 minute.
3. Add the lemon rind and spring onions. Stir-fry for 30 seconds.
4. Sprinkle in the wine or sherry, sugar and soy sauce. When the mixture comes to the boil, stir in the cornflour mixture. Return the chicken to the pan and cook, stirring, for 1 minute. Sprinkle in the lemon juice and serve hot. ·8·12·

Cook's Tip:
In Chinese cooking the emphasis is on the preparation of food rather than cooking. This is the time-consuming part of the recipe – cooking time is very short. Take care to cut ingredients a similar size so that they cook evenly.

Fish and Bean Curd Casserole

Metric/Imperial

500 g/1 lb fish steak (cod, haddock or salmon)
1½ tablespoons flour
2 cakes bean curd
oil for stir-frying
3-4 Chinese dried mushrooms, soaked in warm water for
   20 minutes, squeezed dry, stemmed and chopped
1 teaspoon salt
1 teaspoon sugar
1 tablespoon soy sauce
2 tablespoons rice wine or dry sherry
2 spring onions, chopped
2 slices root ginger, peeled and chopped
300 ml/½ pint clear stock (page 31)
fresh coriander leaves or parsley sprigs, to garnish

1. Cut the fish into about 4 pieces and coat them with the flour.
2. Cut up each cake of bean curd into approximately 8 pieces.
3. Heat the oil in a wok and stir-fry the fish pieces over a moderate heat for 5 minutes or until golden. Remove and drain on absorbent kitchen paper. Set aside until required.
4. In the same oil, fry the bean curd pieces until golden, turning once or twice gently. Remove and drain on absorbent kitchen paper.
5. Place the bean curd, fish pieces and mushrooms in a flameproof casserole or a Chinese sand-pot (or saucepan). Add the salt, sugar, soy sauce, wine or sherry, spring onions, ginger root and the stock. Bring to the boil, then reduce the heat, cover and simmer very gently for 10 minutes. Garnish with fresh coriander or parsley and serve in the casserole. ·3·4·8·

Lemon chicken

Hot-tossed Vegetables

Metric/Imperial

3 1/2 tablespoons oil
1 onion, thinly sliced
3 garlic cloves, peeled and crushed
2 slices root ginger, peeled and shredded
1 1/2 teaspoons salt
1/2 green pepper, cored, seeded and cut into matchstick strips
1/2 red pepper, cored, seeded and cut into matchstick strips
1/4 medium cucumber, cut into matchstick strips
2 celery sticks, cut into 3.5 cm/1 1/2 inch lengths
2 spring onions, cut into 3.5 cm/1 1/2 inch lengths
3-4 lettuce leaves, chopped
250 g/8 oz bean sprouts
1 1/2 teaspoons sugar
2 tablespoons soy sauce
2 tablespoons clear stock (page 31)
1 tablespoon lemon juice
1 tablespoon sesame seed oil

1. Heat the oil in a large wok over a moderate heat. Add the onion, garlic, root ginger and salt, and stir-fry for 30 seconds.
2. Add all the other vegetables. Increase the heat to high, stir and turn the vegetables until they are well coated.
3. Sprinkle with the sugar, soy sauce and stock. Stir-fry for 1 1/2 minutes. Sprinkle with the lemon juice and sesame seed oil and stir once more. Serve hot. ·2·

Meat Cubes in Bean Sauce

Metric/Imperial

500 g/1 lb pork fillet
1 tablespoon cornflour
oil for deep-frying
Sauce:
3 tablespoons yellow bean sauce
3 tablespoons sugar

1. Cut the meat into 1 cm/1/2 inch cubes. Mix the cornflour with enough water to make a fairly thick paste and coat the meat cubes in it.
2. Heat the oil in a wok and, when hot, deep-fry the meat until lightly coloured. Remove with a slotted spoon and drain.
3. Pour off the excess oil, leaving about 1 tablespoon in the wok. Heat the oil until hot, then add the yellow bean sauce combined with the sugar, stir a few times until it starts to bubble, then add the meat and blend well. When each cube is completely coated with the sauce, arrange neatly on a serving dish and serve. ·8·

C · O · U · N · T · D · O · W · N

On the day:

Prepare the chicken, fish, if using, vegetables and garnish; cover and refrigerate. Soak the dried mushrooms for 20 minutes before draining, stemming and shredding for the Lemon Chicken, the fish casserole and the soup. Prepare the stock for the soup, if necessary. Cool, cover and refrigerate until required.

To serve at 8.00 pm:

7.30: Coat the pork cubes in yellow bean paste and deep-fry them. Drain. Mix with the sauce, cover and keep warm over a low heat. Put the rice on to cook and bring the stock for the soup to the boil, if necessary.

7.40: Fry the fish and then the bean curd for the casserole. Place in the sand-pot or saucepan with the remaining ingredients and leave to simmer gently for 10 minutes. If serving the soup, complete and leave on a low heat.

7.50: Check the rice and remove it from the heat if cooked. Set it aside, covered for 10 minutes. Stir-fry the Hot-tossed Vegetables and the Lemon Chicken simultaneously.

8.00: Transfer the food to heated serving dishes, fluffing up the rice with a fork. Add the garnishes and serve immediately.

M·E·N·U

· 2 ·

Vegetarian Lunch for 4

Stir-fried Spinach and Bean Curd
Braised Broccoli or
Stir-fried Mixed Vegetables
Aubergine with Sichuan 'Fish Sauce'
Celery Salad
Plain Boiled Rice
Egg-drop Soup (optional)
·
Date Crisps

You don't have to be a vegetarian to enjoy this menu. The glowing colours of the stir-fried vegetables will stimulate the most jaded of appetites and the unusual aubergine dish will have all your guests clamouring for second helpings. Don't be fooled by the 'fish sauce' in the title – in China this sauce is more commonly served with seafood, hence its name.

The Art of Stir-frying

This is a very rapid method of cooking which seals in all the natural juices. The ingredients are added to a little hot oil, then stirred and tossed constantly for a short time with long chopsticks or a long-handled wooden spoon. Vegetables must be as fresh as possible for this treatment and should be washed before cutting to reduce vitamin loss. All stir-fried dishes should be served immediately, while they are crisp and crunchy. Avoid overcooking and do not put a lid on the wok or pan, or the vegetables will lose their brightness.

To round off the meal, serve delicious date crisps with China tea.

Stir-fried Spinach and Bean Curd

Metric/Imperial
250 g/8 oz spinach
2 cakes bean curd
4 tablespoons oil
1 teaspoon salt
1 teaspoon sugar
1 tablespoon soy sauce
1 teaspoon sesame seed oil, to garnish

1. Wash the spinach well, shaking off the excess water.
2. Cut each bean curd into about 8 pieces.
3. Heat the oil in a wok, fry the bean curd pieces until they are golden, turning them over once or twice gently. Remove with a slotted spoon, drain on absorbent kitchen paper and set aside.
4. Stir-fry the spinach in the remaining oil for about 30 seconds or until the leaves are limp. Add the bean curd pieces, salt, sugar and soy sauce, blend well and cook together for another 1-1½ minutes. Garnish with the sesame seed oil and serve hot.

Braised Broccoli

Metric/Imperial
500 g/1 lb broccoli or cauliflower
3 tablespoons oil
1 teaspoon salt
1 teaspoon sugar
3 tablespoons clear stock (page 31)

1. Cut the broccoli or cauliflower into florets, do not discard the stalks but peel off the tough skin.
2. Heat the oil in a wok and stir-fry the broccoli or cauliflower for about 30 seconds. Add the salt, sugar and stock and stir for 2-3 minutes at the most. Serve hot. ·7·

Stir-fried Mixed Vegetables

Metric/Imperial
3 tablespoons oil
125 g/4 oz bamboo shoots, thinly sliced
125 g/4 oz mangetout, topped and tailed or broccoli, thinly sliced
125 g/4 oz carrots, thinly sliced
125 g/4 oz bean sprouts
1 teaspoon salt
1 teaspoon sugar
1 tablespoon clear stock (page 31)

1. Heat the oil in a wok. Add the bamboo shoots, mangetout or broccoli and carrots. Stir-fry for about 1 minute, then add the bean sprouts with the salt and sugar. Stir-fry for another minute or so, then add some stock if necessary. Do not overcook otherwise the vegetables will lose their colour and crunchiness. Serve hot. ·1·4·

Aubergine with Sichuan 'Fish Sauce'

Metric/Imperial
4-6 dried red chillis
500 g/1 lb aubergines
oil for stir-frying
3-4 spring onions, finely chopped
1 slice root ginger, peeled and finely chopped
1 clove garlic, peeled and finely chopped
1 teaspoon sugar
1 tablespoon soy sauce
1 tablespoon vinegar
1 tablespoon chilli bean paste
2 teaspoons cornflour mixed with 2 tablespoons water
To Garnish:
1 teaspoon sesame seed oil

1. Soak the dried red chillis for 5-10 minutes, then cut them into small pieces discarding the stalks (or leave them whole if small). Peel the aubergines and discard the stalks, then cut them into diamond-shaped chunks.

2. Heat the oil in a wok and stir-fry the aubergines for about 1½-2 minutes or until soft. Scoop out with a slotted spoon and drain.

3. Pour off the oil and return the aubergines to the wok. Add the red chillis, spring onions, root ginger and garlic, stir a few times, then add the sugar, soy sauce, vinegar and chilli bean paste and continue stirring for about 1 minute. Finally add the cornflour and water mixture, blend together well and garnish with the sesame seed oil. Leave to cool completely and serve cold. ·6·

Stir-fried mixed vegetables; Braised broccoli; Aubergine with Sichuan 'fish sauce'; Spinach and bean curd

Celery Salad

Metric/Imperial
1 celery stick
1 small green pepper, cored and seeded
1 teaspoon salt
2 litres/4 pints water
Dressing:
2 tablespoons soy sauce
1 tablespoon vinegar
1 tablespoon sesame seed oil
1 slice root ginger, peeled and finely shredded, to garnish

1. Thinly slice the celery diagonally. Thinly slice the green pepper. Place them both in a pan of boiling, salted water for 1 to 2 minutes. Pour into a colander and rinse in cold water. Drain.

2. Mix together the ingredients for the dressing and pour it over the celery and green pepper, toss well, then garnish and serve. ·14·

Plain Boiled Rice

Metric/Imperial
350 g/12 oz long-grain rice
750 ml/1¼ pints water

1. Wash and rinse the rice in cold water. Bring a pan of water to the boil, add the rice and bring it back to the boil. Cover the pan tightly with a lid and reduce the heat. Cook over a gentle heat for about 20 minutes.
2. It is best not to serve the rice immediately but to leave it in the covered pan for 10 minutes. This ensures that the rice is not too sticky. Fluff it up with a fork or spoon before serving.

Cook's Tip:
Should you prefer your rice to be softer and less fluffy, then use the rounded, pudding rice and reduce the amount of water by a quarter.

Egg-drop Soup

Metric/Imperial
2 eggs
1 teaspoon salt
600 ml/1 pint vegetable stock
2 teaspoons finely chopped spring onion or chives,
*   to garnish*

1. Beat the eggs together with a small pinch of the salt.
2. Bring the stock to the boil, pour the beaten eggs in very slowly, stirring constantly.
3. Place the remaining salt and spring onions in a serving bowl, pour in the soup and serve hot.

Date Crisps

Metric/Imperial
30 jujubes or dates, stoned
30 walnut halves

30 wonton skins
1½ tablespoons brown sugar
oil for deep-frying
3 tablespoons icing sugar

1. Fill each date with a walnut half. Place each date on a wonton wrapping and add a pinch of sugar. Moisten the edges of the wrappings, roll and seal by twisting the ends.
2. Heat the oil to 160°C/325°F. Deep-fry the rolls until golden brown; do not overcook.
3. Drain on absorbent kitchen paper and sprinkle with icing sugar. Allow to cool before serving.

C · O · U · N · T · D · O · W · N

On the day or day before:
Make the stock for the soup, if necessary. Cool, cover and refrigerate. Prepare all the vegetables except the spinach and make the garnishes, cover and refrigerate. Prepare the Aubergine with Sichuan 'Fish Sauce' and the Date Crisps. Cover and store in the refrigerator. Make the salad dressing.

To serve at 1.00 pm:
12.15: Remove the completed aubergine dish from the refrigerator and assemble the Celery Salad. Toss and garnish both dishes.
12.30: Put the rice on to cook.
12.40: Start heating the stock for the soup, if serving, and beat the eggs. Cut up the bean curd.
12.50: Take the rice off the heat and set aside, covered, for 10 minutes. Prepare 3 pans or woks and stir-fry the Spinach and Bean Curd, the Braised Broccoli and the Stir-fried Mixed Vegetables, if using, simultaneously. Transfer all the food to serving dishes and garnish. Fluff up the rice with a fork.
1.00: Add the eggs to the soup and serve immediately with the other dishes.

Cook's Tip:
Never use canned bean sprouts for stir-frying, they have no crunch. If fresh sprouts are not available use thinly shredded celery sticks instead.

MENU

· 3 ·

Southern Chinese Supper for 4

Curried Chicken with Coconut Juice
Soya-braised Fish Steaks
Pork Spare Ribs in Sweet and Sour Sauce
Chinese Cabbage and Mushrooms
Plain Boiled Rice (page 12)
Shrimp Wonton Soup (optional)

The dishes on this menu come from Canton, in Southern China, a region which has for centuries been famous for its sophisticated and varied cuisine. Cantonese cooks have access to the finest ingredients. Vegetables and fruit flourish in the lush climate, and sugar cane grows in the valleys, its influence apparent in the many sweetmeats popular in this region. Cantonese meals are colourful, with much emphasis on stir-fried vegetables. Unlike the food of its neighbour, Sichuan, Cantonese cooking is not particularly spicy, but specialises in more subtle flavours, including their famous and often imitated sweet and sour sauces. One of these sauces features in this menu, where it is served with spare ribs of pork. Other dishes include a lightly curried chicken dish with coconut juice, and soya-braised fish steaks.

Wonton Wrappings

The delicious shrimp soup which can be served with this menu could easily be interchanged with soup recipes in other menus. It introduces wontons, edible wrappings that encase sweet or savoury fillings and may be used in soups or braised dishes, or simply deep-fried. They are available from most Chinese stores and if you have any left over after preparing this menu, try them in Date Crisps (see page 12).

Curried Chicken with Coconut Juice

Metric/Imperial

2 tablespoons oil
1 × 1 kg/2 lb chicken, cut into serving pieces
1 tablespoon rice wine or dry sherry
1 teaspoon salt
pinch of pepper
2 tablespoons soy sauce
2 onions, cut into quarters
3 spring onions, chopped
3 garlic cloves, peeled and chopped
2 tablespoons curry paste
2 teaspoons curry powder
300 ml/½ pint clear stock (page 31)
3 potatoes, cut into 2.5 cm/1 inch pieces
2 carrots, cut into 2.5 cm/1 inch pieces
4 tablespoons coconut juice

2 tablespoons plain flour
2 teaspoons sugar
few strips of green pepper, to garnish

1. Heat 1 tablespoon of the oil in a wok. Add the chicken and stir-fry until lightly browned. Add the wine or sherry and soy sauce. Season with the salt and pepper. Stir-fry for 2 seconds, then add the onions. Stir-fry for 30 seconds, then transfer the mixture to a large saucepan.
2. Heat the remaining oil in the wok. Add the spring onions and garlic and stir-fry for 4-5 seconds. Add the curry paste and curry powder. Stir-fry for 30 seconds, then stir in the stock.
3. Pour this sauce over the chicken and add the potatoes and carrots. Bring to the boil, cover and simmer for 20 minutes, until tender.
4. Combine the coconut juice with the flour and sugar and stir into the pan. Cook, stirring, until the sauce is thickened. Garnish and serve hot. ·1·8·

Shrimp wonton soup

Soya-braised Fish Steaks

Metric/Imperial
50 g/2 oz lard
3-4 spring onions, finely chopped
2-3 slices root ginger, peeled and finely chopped
500 g/1 lb cod or halibut fillets, quartered
2 tablespoons rice wine or dry sherry
2 tablespoons soy sauce
1 tablespoon sugar
125 ml/4 fl oz water
1 tablespoon cornflour, dissolved in 1½ tablespoons water
1 teaspoon sesame seed oil
shredded spring onion, to garnish

1. Melt the lard in a wok over high heat. Add the spring onions and root ginger and stir-fry for a few seconds.
2. Add the fish pieces and stir very gently to separate.
3. Add the wine or sherry and bring to the boil, then stir in the soy sauce, sugar and water. Simmer for about 10 minutes.
4. Add the cornflour mixture and simmer, stirring, until thickened and smooth. Add the sesame seed oil and serve immediately, garnished with shredded spring onion.

Cook's Tip:
When stir-frying, choose the freshest vegetables you can find: do not leave them lying around too long before use and always wash vegetables before cutting them in order to avoid losing vitamins in the water.

Cook vegetables as soon as you have cut them, so that not too much of the vitamin content is destroyed by exposure to the air.

Never overcook the vegetables, nor use too much water in cooking. Avoid using a lid over the wok or pan unless specified, as it will spoil the brightness of the colour.

Pork Spare Ribs in Sweet and Sour Sauce

Metric/Imperial
500 g/1 lb pork spare ribs, cut into serving pieces
½ teaspoon salt
freshly ground Sichuan or black pepper
1 teaspoon sugar
1 egg yolk
1 tablespoon cornflour
1 small green pepper, cored and seeded
1 small red pepper, cored and seeded
2 tablespoons plain flour
oil for deep-frying
Sauce:
1 tablespoon soy sauce
3 tablespoons sugar
3 tablespoons vinegar
1 tablespoon cornflour mixed with 3 tablespoons water

1. Place the pork in a bowl and add the salt, pepper, sugar, egg yolk and cornflour. Mix well together and leave to marinate for about 10 minutes. Thinly shred the green and red peppers.
2. Coat each spare rib piece in plain flour. Heat the oil in a wok until hot, then turn down the heat to low and let the oil cool a little. Put the spare ribs in the oil piece by piece, so that they do not stick together, separating them with chopsticks if necessary. Increase the heat after a while and fry until crisp and golden. Remove with a slotted spoon.
3. Heat the oil until bubbling and fry the spare ribs once more for about 30 seconds, or until golden brown. Remove with a slotted spoon and drain.
4. Pour off the excess oil, leaving about 1 tablespoon in the wok and stir-fry the green and red peppers for a few seconds. Add the soy sauce, sugar and vinegar, stir a few times, then add the cornflour mixed with water. When the sauce becomes a smooth paste, put in the spare ribs and blend well.

Chinese Cabbage and Mushrooms

Metric/Imperial

6-8 Chinese dried mushrooms, soaked in warm water for
*   20 minutes, squeezed dry, stemmed and chopped*
500 g/1 lb Chinese cabbage leaves
3 tablespoons oil
1 teaspoon salt
1 teaspoon sugar
1 tablespoon soy sauce
1 teaspoon sesame seed oil

1. Reserve the soaking liquid from the mushrooms. Roughly chop the cabbage leaves.
2. Heat the oil in a wok and stir-fry the cabbage and the mushrooms until soft, about 3 minutes. Add the salt, sugar and soy sauce and cook for a further 1½ minutes. Stir in a little of the water in which the mushrooms soaked, then add the sesame seed oil and serve immediately. ·14·

Shrimp Wonton Soup

Metric/Imperial

40 sheets wonton wrappings
1.2 litres/2 pints hot clear stock (page 31)
1 spring onion, chopped
Filling:
1 egg
1 teaspoon rice wine or dry sherry
1 teaspoon salt
pinch of pepper
2 teaspoons oil
½ teaspoon sugar
1 tablespoon cornflour
250 g/8 oz prawns, shelled, de-veined and
*   finely chopped*
125 g/4 oz fresh or canned water chestnuts,
*   drained and chopped*

1. For the filling, combine the egg, wine or sherry, salt, pepper, oil, sugar and cornflour in a bowl. Add the prawns and water chestnuts and stir until the mixture holds together.
2. Place ½ teaspoon filling in the centre of each wonton wrapping. Moisten the edges with water, fold corner to corner into a triangle and seal. Then seal the bottom corners.
3. Fill a saucepan with water and bring to the boil. Add the wonton, a few at a time, and cook until they float to the surface. Lift out with a slotted spoon and place in the hot stock in another saucepan. Keep hot while cooking the remaining wonton.
4. Sprinkle with the spring onion. Serve hot.

C · O · U · N · T · D · O · W · N

On the day:
Prepare the chicken, pork spare ribs, fish, vegetables and garnishes. Cover and refrigerate. Soak the dried mushrooms. Prepare the filling for the wonton.

To serve at 8.00 pm:
7.00: Wrap the wonton filling in the wrappings and cook in water, transferring to the stock when cooked. Keep hot over a low heat.
7.15: Marinate the spare ribs.
7.20: Prepare the Curried Chicken with Coconut Juice and leave to simmer as directed.
7.30: Fry the spare ribs and set aside in a warm place. Combine the ingredients for the sauce. Cook the rice.
7.40: Make the Soya-braised Fish Steaks, if using, and leave to simmer. Complete the chicken and place the spare ribs in the sauce to heat through.
7.50: Add the cornflour mixture to the Fish Steaks and heat through. Cook the cabbage and mushrooms.
8.00: Transfer all food to serving dishes and serve immediately.

Cook's Tip:
Soy sauce: Sold in bottles or cans, this most popular Chinese sauce is used both for cooking and at the table. Whenever possible, and unless otherwise stated, use *light soy sauce* which has more flavour.

M·E·N·U

· 4 ·

Northern Chinese Meal for 4-6

Red-cooked Whole Carp
Bean Curd with Pork and Cabbage
Mixed Chinese Vegetables
Lamb with Spring Onions
Braised Beef
Plain Boiled Rice (page 12)
Chicken and Mushroom Soup

Travel north in China, and as the countryside changes, so does the cuisine. In Peking, where this menu originated, the food tends to be light rather than rich, and it is always extremely elegantly presented. Much of the flavouring is subtle, and many ingredients are selected for texture rather than taste, as is the case with the wood ears in the fish dish. Wood ears are fungi which are crisp yet slippery; they are also known as cloud ears and must always be soaked and rinsed before use. Another interesting texture is provided by Chinese cabbage, the most widely-used green vegetable of this region, which has a flavour reminiscent of cabbage, lettuce and celery. It is used here with pork and bean curd.

Bean Curd

This is a custard-like preparation of puréed and pressed soya beans, which is exceptionally high in protein. If covered with water it will keep in a refrigerator for several days. Freezing it, as in the pork and cabbage dish, leads to the formation of small holes in the curd. When it is later thawed and added to the dish, the juices can therefore permeate throughout the curd. Do not freeze the bean curd for more than 12 hours or it will toughen.

C · H · I · N · E · S · E

Red-cooked Whole Carp

Metric/Imperial
1 kg/2 lb whole carp, cleaned and scaled
4 tablespoons soy sauce
3 tablespoons oil
15 g/½ oz dried wood ears, soaked in warm water for
   20 minutes, squeezed dry and stemmed
50 g/2 oz canned bamboo shoots, drained and sliced
3-4 spring onions, shredded
3 slices root ginger, shredded
2 teaspoons cornflour, dissolved in 1 tablespoon water
Sauce:
2 tablespoons soy sauce
2 tablespoons rice wine or dry sherry
2 teaspoons sugar
4 tablespoons clear stock (page 31)

1. Make diagonal slashes across the fish on both sides. Marinate the fish in the soy sauce for at least 30 minutes. Mix together the sauce ingredients.
2. Heat the oil in a wok. When it is very hot, add the fish and fry until golden on both sides. Add the sauce, wood ears and bamboo shoots and continue cooking for about 20 minutes.
3. Add the spring onions and root ginger and cook until the sauce is reduced by half.
4. Add the cornflour mixture and cook, stirring, until thickened. Transfer to a serving dish. Pour over the sauce and serve hot. ·9·

Bean Curd with Pork and Cabbage

Metric/Imperial
1 cake bean curd, cut into 3.5 cm/1½ inch squares
3 tablespoons oil
250 g/8 oz lean pork, cut into thin bite-sized pieces
1 spring onion, chopped
2 slices root ginger, chopped
2 teaspoons salt
1 tablespoon rice wine or dry sherry
1 litre/1¾ pints clear stock (page 31)
500 g/1 lb Chinese cabbage, shredded

1. Freeze the bean curd squares overnight. Thaw in hot water, then drain.
2. Heat the oil in a wok. Add the pork, spring onion, root ginger and bean curd and stir-fry until the meat is lightly browned. Add the salt, wine or sherry and stock and bring to the boil. Cover and simmer for 10 minutes.
3. Add the cabbage and simmer until it is tender; about 10 minutes. Serve hot. ·3·

Mixed Chinese Vegetables

Metric/Imperial
1 small cauliflower, divided into florets
6 Chinese dried mushrooms, soaked in warm water for
   20 minutes, squeezed dry, stemmed and sliced. Reserve
   the soaking liquid
2 tablespoons oil
8 water chestnuts, cut into large pieces
2 tablespoons cornflour
2 tablespoons soy sauce
2 tablespoons rice wine or dry sherry
2 tablespoons stock

1. Cover the cauliflower florets with boiling water and leave for 5 minutes, then drain.
2. Heat the oil in a wok. Stir-fry the mushrooms for 2-3 minutes over a high heat. Add the chestnuts and cauliflower, mix well and cook for approximately 2 minutes.
3. Mix the cornflour to a smooth paste with the remaining ingredients and add the mushroom liquid. Add to the pan and bring to the boil, stirring, until the mixture is thickened and smooth. Cook for 2-3 minutes and serve immediately in a warmed serving dish. ·1·2·

Lamb with Spring Onions

Metric/Imperial

2 tablespoons soy sauce
1/2 teaspoon salt
1 tablespoon rice wine or dry sherry
125 ml/4 fl oz oil
250 g/8 oz lean lamb, very thinly sliced
1 tablespoon red wine vinegar
1 tablespoon sesame seed oil
1/2 teaspoon freshly ground Sichuan or black peppercorns
2 garlic cloves, peeled and crushed
2 bunches spring onions

1. Mix together 1 tablespoon of the soy sauce, the salt, wine or sherry and 2 tablespoons of the oil. Add the lamb slices and leave to marinate.
2. Mix the remaining soy sauce with the vinegar, sesame seed oil and pepper in a small bowl.
3. Heat the remaining oil in a wok. Add the garlic and stir-fry for 10 seconds. Add the meat and stir-fry until browned. Shred a few of the spring onions and set aside for garnish. Cut the remainder into 5 cm/ 2 inch pieces and add to the meat together with the vinegar mixture. Stir-fry for a few seconds. Serve hot, garnished with the reserved spring onions.

Cook's Tip:

Fresh bean curd sealed in a small container packaged under the name *tofu* is the Japanese variety. It is extremely soft and silky but does not absorb other flavours as readily as the firmer Chinese sort. Also it tends to fall apart in stir-frying, therefore it is not suitable for Chinese cooking, except for soup recipes. Blanching bean-curd for 2-3 minutes will harden the texture, so that it will not fall apart so easily.

Freezing bean-curd will give it a honeycomb and slightly tough texture, it is then more suitable for the slow, long-cooking methods.

Bean curd with pork and cabbage; Lamb with spring onions

Braised Beef

Metric/Imperial
750 g/1½-1¾ lb shin of beef
2 tablespoons rice wine or dry sherry
2 tablespoons soy sauce
1 teaspoon five-spice powder
2 slices root ginger
250 g/8 oz tomatoes, halved or quartered
50 g/2 oz demerara brown sugar
250 g/8 oz carrots, peeled and diced
1 teaspoon salt
flat-leaf parsley, to garnish

1. Cut the beef into 4 cm/1½ inch cubes and trim off any excess fat, but leave the sinew in the meat as it will give the liquid extra flavour and richness.
2. Place the meat in a saucepan with enough water to cover, add the wine or sherry, soy sauce, five-spice powder, root ginger and tomatoes.
3. Bring to the boil, then reduce the heat, cover and simmer for 45 minutes. Add the sugar and cook for a further 30 minutes.
4. Add the carrots with the salt to the beef and cook for a further 30 minutes until the liquid has reduced and thickened into a delicious sauce, increasing the heat if necessary. Serve hot garnished with parsley.

Chicken and Mushroom Soup

Metric/Imperial
125 g/4 oz chicken breast meat, skinned and boned
salt
2 teaspoons cornflour
1 egg white
50 g/2 oz mushrooms
50 g/2 oz bamboo shoots
600 ml/1 pint clear stock (page 31)
1 tablespoon soy sauce

1. Thinly slice the chicken breast meat, mix with a pinch of salt, the cornflour and egg white. Cut the mushrooms and bamboo shoots into thin slices.
2. Bring the stock to the boil, add the chicken, mushrooms and bamboo shoots, then add the soy sauce. When the soup starts to boil again it is ready to serve.

C · O · U · N · T · D · O · W · N
On the day:
Early in the morning, freeze the bean curd for the pork dish. Prepare the fish, pork, lamb or beef, if using, and vegetables and garnishes. Cover and refrigerate. Make the stock for the soup, if necessary. Soak the wood ears for the fish dish and the mushrooms for the Mixed Chinese Vegetables.
To serve at 8.00 pm:
6.15: Start cooking the Braised Beef, if using.
6.45: Marinate the lamb and the fish. In separate bowls, mix the lamb and fish sauces. Thaw the bean curd.
7.00: Add the sugar to the Braised Beef and continue cooking.
7.15: Fry the whole fish, then leave to cook in the prepared sauce.
7.30: Prepare the Bean Curd with Pork and Cabbage and simmer for 10 minutes as directed. Put the rice on to boil and add the carrots to the beef. Blanch the cauliflower and prepare the mushrooms for the Mixed Chinese Vegetables.
7.40: Add the cabbage to the Bean Curd with Pork and continue to simmer. Add the spring onions and ginger to the fish. Complete the Mixed Chinese Vegetables and leave on low heat. Put the stock on to boil for the soup.
7.50: Stir-fry the Lamb with Spring Onions and complete the Red-cooked Whole Carp. Take the rice off the heat and set aside, covered for 10 minutes. Finish the soup.
8.00: Transfer the food to serving dishes, fluff up the rice, garnish and serve immediately.

M·E·N·U

· 5 ·

Eastern Chinese Feast for 6

Stir-fried Prawns
Red-cooked Beef with Broccoli
Shanghai 'Smoked' Fish
Braised Bamboo Shoots
Yangchow 'Lion's Head'
Fried Rice (page 44)

·

Steamed Dumplings with Sweet Filling

Pride of place on this menu must go to 'Lion's Head', a famous dish that originated in Yangchow on the Yangtze river delta in Eastern China. The pork meatballs are supposed to resemble the shape of a lion's head, and the cabbage to look like its mane, hence the name. For a busy hostess, the dish has the advantage that it can be prepared well in advance of the meal and the long, slow cooking process gives her time to concentrate on the rest of this elaborate but quite straightforward menu, which also features stir-fried prawns, braised bamboo shoots and the interesting Shanghai 'Smoked' Fish, which is not quite what it seems. The fried rice on the menu is optional – serve it only if you know your guests have hearty appetites. The Chinese strongly believe that the greater the variety – the more successful the meal!

Sweet Surprise

The meal concludes on a sugary note, with steamed dumplings – unusual on a Chinese menu but typical of this region where a fondness for sweet dishes and a considerable Western influence combine to produce some delectable desserts.

Stir-fried Prawns

Metric/Imperial

1 tablespoon rice wine or dry sherry
1 egg white
salt
freshly ground black pepper
4 teaspoons cornflour
500 g/1 lb prawns or shrimps, shelled and de-veined
7 tablespoons oil
1/2 teaspoon finely chopped garlic
1 teaspoon soy sauce
1 teaspoon tomato paste
1 teaspoon sugar
1 teaspoon red wine vinegar
1 tablespoon water (optional)
flat-leaf parsley or coriander, to garnish

Braised bamboo shoots

1. Mix together the wine or sherry, egg white, a pinch of salt, pinch of pepper and 1 tablespoon of the cornflour in a bowl. Add the prawns and turn to coat with the mixture.
2. Heat 5 tablespoons of the oil in a wok. Add the prawns and stir-fry until they are no longer opaque. Transfer to a plate.
3. Add the remaining oil to the wok and heat. Add the garlic, soy sauce and tomato paste and stir-fry for 1 minute.
4. Return the prawns to the wok with the sugar, vinegar and salt and pepper to taste. Stir a few times. If necessary, thicken with the remaining cornflour dissolved in the water. Stir into the wok and cook over a high heat for a further minute.

Red-cooked Beef with Broccoli

Metric/Imperial
500 g/1 lb shin of beef, cubed
750 g/1 1/2 lb brisket of beef, cubed
4-5 slices root ginger, peeled and chopped
1 teaspoon salt
1/2 teaspoon peppercorns
3 tablespoons soy sauce
600 ml/1 pint water
300 ml/1/2 pint white wine
1 chicken stock cube
500 g/1 lb broccoli, broken into florets

1. Blanch the beef cubes in boiling water for 2 minutes and drain. Put the beef in a large pan. Add the root ginger, salt, peppercorns, soy sauce and water. Bring to the boil, then cover and simmer gently for 2 hours, stirring occasionally.
2. Add the wine and stock cube. Simmer for 1 hour. Add the broccoli and cook for 10 minutes.
3. Drain most of the cooking liquor into a bowl. Transfer the meat to a serving bowl and arrange the broccoli around the edge. Serve the reserved liquor as a soup to accompany the meal. ·4·

Shanghai 'Smoked' Fish

Metric/Imperial
750 g/1 1/2 lb cod or haddock cutlets
3 tablespoons soy sauce
3 tablespoons rice wine or dry sherry
1/2 teaspoon salt
3-4 spring onions
3 slices root ginger, peeled
1 teaspoon five-spice powder
4 tablespoons sugar
125 ml/4 fl oz water
oil for deep-frying

1. Leave the fish cutlets in fairly large pieces, otherwise they will break up when cooked. Combine the soy sauce, wine or sherry and salt and marinate the fish for 5-10 minutes.
2. Remove the fish from the marinade. Bring the marinade to the boil in a saucepan over a moderate heat with the spring onions, root ginger, five-spice powder, sugar and water. Simmer gently for about 10 minutes, then strain through a sieve, reserving the sauce.
3. Heat the oil in a wok until fairly hot. Deep-fry the fish pieces for about 4-5 minutes or until they are crisp and golden. Remove with a perforated spoon and dip them in the sauce for 10 minutes or so before laying them out side by side on a plate to cool. The remainder of the sauce can be stored in the refrigerator for 3-4 weeks and used again. ·10·11·12·

Braised Bamboo Shoots

Metric/Imperial
300 g/10 oz bamboo shoots
3 tablespoons oil
2 spring onions, finely chopped
4-5 Chinese dried mushrooms, soaked in warm water for 20 minutes, squeezed dry, stemmed and sliced.
1 tablespoon rice wine or dry sherry
1 tablespoon soy sauce
2 teaspoons cornflour
50 g/2 oz ham, finely chopped, to garnish

1. Cut the bamboo shoots into strips.
2. Heat the oil in a wok, add the spring onions, mushrooms and bamboo shoots and stir-fry for about 1 minute, then add the wine or sherry and soy sauce. Continue to cook for a further minute, adding a little stock if necessary.
3. Mix the cornflour with a little cold water and add to the wok, stirring until the juices are thickened and smooth. Serve immediately, garnished with the finely chopped ham. ·6·

Yangchow 'Lion's Head'

Metric/Imperial
500 g/1 lb pork, not too lean
2 slices root ginger, peeled and finely chopped
2 spring onions, finely chopped
2 teaspoons salt
2 tablespoons rice wine or dry sherry
1 tablespoon cornflour
1 Chinese cabbage
2 tablespoons oil
300 ml/1/2 pint clear stock (page 31)

1. Finely mince or chop the pork, mix with the root ginger, spring onions, salt, wine or sherry and cornflour. Shape the mixture into 4-6 meatballs.
2. Cut the cabbage into large chunks. Heat the oil in a wok, then stir-fry the cabbage for about 1 minute. Place the meatballs on top and add the stock, bring to the boil, then cover and simmer gently for 45 minutes. Serve hot.

Steamed Dumplings with Sweet Filling

Metric/Imperial
Pastry:
1 1/2 tablespoons dried yeast
2 1/2 teaspoons sugar
3 tablespoons lukewarm water
500 g/1 lb plain flour
300 ml/1/2 pint lukewarm milk
Filling:
1 × 250 g/8 oz can sweetened chestnut purée or yellow bean sauce

1. Dissolve the yeast and sugar in the water. Sift the flour into a large bowl, then gradually stir in the yeast mixture and the milk. Mix to a firm dough. Turn the dough onto a lightly floured surface and knead well for at least 5 minutes. Transfer to a bowl, cover with a damp cloth and leave in a warm place for 1 1/2 hours or until doubled in size.
2. Knead the dough on a lightly floured surface for about 5 minutes, then roll into a long sausage shape 5 cm/2 inches in diameter. Slice with a sharp knife into 2.5 cm/1 inch rounds. Flatten each round with the palm of your hand, then roll out to circles 10 cm/4 inches in diameter.
3. Place 1 teaspoon chestnut purée or bean sauce in the centre of each round, then gather up the dough around the filling to meet at the top. Twist the top. Leave to rest for at least 20 minutes.
4. Place the dumplings on a damp cloth in the bottom of a steamer, leaving a 2.5 cm/1 inch space between each one. Steam for 20 minutes. Serve hot.

C · O · U · N · T · D · O · W · N

On the day:
Prepare all the meat, fish, if using, vegetables and garnish. If required, cook the rice for the Fried Rice. Cover and refrigerate. Make the Shanghai 'Smoked' Fish, if using, and refrigerate. Shape the 'Lion's Heads', and keep, covered, in the refrigerator. Soak the mushrooms.

To serve at 8.00 pm:
4.30: Blanch the beef cubes, add the sauce ingredients, bring to the boil and cook as directed. Make the dough for the Sweet Dumplings and refrigerate.
6.45: Add the wine and stock cube to the beef and continue cooking. Fill and shape the dumplings, cover and refrigerate.
7.00: Prepare the Yangchow 'Lion's Head' and leave to simmer.
7.40: Cook the ham, prawns and peas for the Fried Rice. Add the broccoli to the beef then braise the bamboo shoots and stir-fry the prawns.
7.50: Complete the Fried Rice if serving.
8.00: Transfer all dishes to serving plates and garnish and serve. Put the sweet dumplings on to steam while the first course is being served.

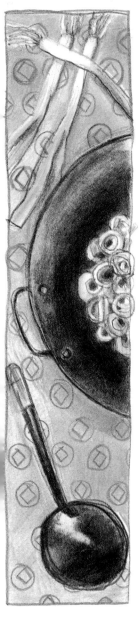

M·E·N·U

· 6 ·

Impressive Dinner for 4

Stir-fried Kidney-flowers Shandong-style
Cantonese Soya-braised Chicken
Rapid-fried Lamb Slices
Braised Aubergines
Fried Rice (page 44)

·

Steamed Honey Pears

This menu is a good illustration of how the Chinese extract every ounce of flavour from their ingredients and combine them in such a way as to produce dishes whose taste is sensational. In the recipe for Stir-fried Kidney-flowers Shandong-style, a humdrum ingredient is transformed, and even guests who claim to dislike kidneys will be captivated, not only by the flavour, but also by the appearance of this colourful dish. The kidneys are made to resemble flowers. This is a basic Chinese cooking technique, which is also used for squid, tripe and aubergines, where a criss-cross pattern is scored on the surface of the chosen ingredient.

Soya-braised Chicken

Also on the menu is a Cantonese speciality, Soya-braised Chicken. If this seems familiar, it is because it is the bright brown chicken so often glimpsed in the windows of Chinese restaurants.

Rose Dew

Do try to obtain the Chinese liqueur, Rose Dew, used with the pears. It is called 'Mei Kuei Lu' and is distilled from sorghum and other grains blended with rose petals, and aromatic herbs. It has a superb flavour.

Stir-fried Kidney-flowers Shandong-style

Metric/Imperial

50 g/2 oz bamboo shoots
50 g/2 oz water chestnuts
125 g/4 oz seasonal greens (cabbage, broccoli, spinach or
*   lettuce)*
1 pair pig's kidneys (about 250 g/8 oz)
1 teaspoon salt
1 tablespoon cornflour
oil for deep-frying
1 spring onion, finely chopped
1 slice root ginger, peeled and finely chopped
1 clove garlic, peeled and finely chopped
10 g/¼ oz wood ears, soaked in warm water for
*   20 minutes, squeezed dry, and stemmed*
1 tablespoon rice wine or dry sherry
1 tablespoon vinegar
1½ tablespoons soy sauce
1 teaspoon sesame seed oil
3 tablespoons clear stock (page 31)

1. Cut the bamboo shoots and water chestnuts into small slices. Blanch the green vegetables.
2. Split each kidney in half lengthways and discard the white and dark parts in the middle. Score the surface of each half kidney diagonally in a criss-cross pattern, then cut each half into 6-8 pieces. Mix with ½ teaspoon of the salt and about ½ tablespoon of the cornflour.
3. Heat the oil in a wok. While it is heating, quickly blanch the kidney pieces in a pan of boiling water, strain and pat dry with a clean cloth or absorbent kitchen paper. Deep-fry the kidney pieces in hot oil for a few seconds only, then scoop out with a slotted spoon.
4. Pour off the excess oil, leaving about 1 tablespoon in the wok. Add the spring onion, root ginger and garlic, stirring a few times. Next add the wood ears, bamboo shoots, water chestnuts, kidneys, the remaining salt, the wine or sherry, vinegar, soy sauce and sesame seed oil, stirring constantly for about 1 minute. Finally add the remaining cornflour mixed with the stock and blend well. Serve hot.

Cantonese Soya-braised Chicken

Metric/Imperial

1.5 kg/3-3½ lb roasting chicken
2 tablespoons freshly ground Sichuan or black pepper
2 tablespoons finely chopped root ginger
5 tablespoons dark soy sauce
3 tablespoons rice wine or dry sherry
2 tablespoons sugar
3 tablespoons oil
125 ml/4 fl oz clear stock (page 31)
1 small lettuce

1. Clean the chicken well and dry it thoroughly. Rub both inside and out with the pepper and root ginger.
2. Marinate the chicken in the soy sauce, rice wine or sherry and sugar for at least 45 minutes, turning it over several times.
3. Heat the oil in a wok large enough to hold the whole chicken. Brown it lightly all over, then add the marinade diluted with the stock. Bring it to the boil, reduce the heat, cover and leave to simmer for approximately 45 minutes, turning it over several times during the cooking time. (Use wooden spoons to turn the chicken to make sure the skin does not break).
4. Chop the chicken into small pieces and arrange them neatly on a bed of crisp lettuce leaves, then pour over 2 tablespoons of the sauce to serve when cold. The remainder of the sauce can be stored in the refrigerator for approximately 3-4 weeks and used again. ·9·13·

Rapid-fried Lamb Slices

Metric/Imperial

250-300 g/8-10 oz leg of lamb fillet
about 12 spring onions
4 tablespoons oil
1 tablespoon soy sauce
½ teaspoon salt
1 tablespoon rice wine or dry sherry
½ teaspoon freshly ground Sichuan or black pepper
2 teaspoons cornflour
1 clove garlic, peeled and crushed
1 tablespoon sesame seed oil
1 tablespoon vinegar

1. Trim off all the fat from the lamb and cut it into slices as thin as possible. Cut the spring onions in half lengthways, then slice them diagonally.

2. Marinate both the meat and spring onions in a tablespoon of the oil, the soy sauce, salt, wine or sherry, pepper and cornflour.

3. Heat the remaining oil in a wok until smoking, then add the crushed garlic, lamb and spring onions, stirring constantly over a high heat for a few seconds, and finally add the sesame seed oil and vinegar. Blend well, then serve hot. ·10·

Stir-fried kidney flowers Shandong-style;
Rapid-fried lamb slices

Braised Aubergines

Metric/Imperial
275 g/10 oz aubergines
600 ml/1 pint oil for deep-frying
2 tablespoons soy sauce
1 tablespoon sugar
2 tablespoons clear stock (page 31)
1 teaspoon sesame seed oil

Choose the long, purple variety of aubergine, rather than the large round kind if possible.

1. Discard the stalks and cut the aubergines into diamond-shaped chunks.
2. Heat the oil in a wok until hot and deep-fry the aubergine chunks in batches until golden, then remove with a perforated spoon and drain.
3. Pour off the excess oil, leaving about 1 tablespoon in the wok. Return the aubergines to the pan, add the soy sauce, sugar and the stock. Cook for about 2 minutes over a fairly high heat, adding more stock if necessary and stirring occasionally.
4. When the juice is reduced to almost nothing, add the sesame seed oil, blend well and serve. ·2·3·5·

Steamed Honeyed Pears

Metric/Imperial
4 medium pears, peeled but with stems intact
4 tablespoons sugar
4 tablespoons clear honey
2 tablespoons Chinese rose dew liqueur, cherry brandy or
*   crème de menthe (see introduction)*

1. Stand the pears in a saucepan and just cover with water. Bring to the boil over a low heat and simmer for 30 minutes.
2. Pour off half the water. Sprinkle the pears with the sugar and simmer for another 10 minutes. Remove the pears from the pan and chill in the refrigerator for 2 hours.
3. Pour off half the water remaining in the pan. Add the honey and liqueur to the pan and stir until well blended. Chill the sauce for 2 hours.
4. Arrange the pears in individual dishes. Pour the chilled honey sauce over and serve.

Cook's Tip:
Use firm, even-size pears for this dish. Peel the fruit with a swivel potato peeler.

C · O · U · N · T · D · O · W · N

On the day:
Prepare the meats, vegetables and garnishes. Leave the chicken or lamb, to marinate. Prepare the steamed steamed pears and the honey syrup and refrigerate. Cook the rice, if necessary, for the Fried Rice. Allow the chicken to marinate for at least 45 minutes, then prepare the Soya-braised Chicken and, when cool, chill in the refrigerator.

To serve at 8.00 pm:
7.30: Soak the wood ears for the kidney dish. Arrange the pears on the serving plate and pour the sauce over. Refrigerate until required. Cook the Braised Aubergines.
7.40: Heat the stock for the soup. Scramble the eggs and cook the ham, prawns and peas for the Fried Rice. Cook the Stir-fried Kidney-flowers Shandong-style and the Rapid-fried Lamb Slices, if using and keep warm in a low oven.
7.55: Complete the Fried Rice.
8.00: Transfer the food to serving plates, garnish and serve immediately.

Cook's Tip:
Wood ears, often used in Chinese cooking, are also known as 'cloud ears' and are a dried black fungus. They should always be soaked in warm water for 20 minutes then rinsed before using. They have a crunchy texture and a mild but subtle flavour.

Sesame seed oil is sold in bottles and widely used in China as a garnish rather than for cooking. It has a strong aromatic flavour.

M·E·N·U

· 7 ·

Special Chinese Supper for 6

Chinese Hot-pot
Dan Dan Noodles

·

Walnut Sweet
Almond Jelly with Chow Chow
China Tea

This menu centres on the Chinese Hot-pot or Mongolian Fire-pot, as it is sometimes called. This Northern Chinese speciality makes a stunning and sociable main course at a dinner party. It is rather like a fondue where the actual cooking is done not in the kitchen but on the dining table by each individual.

The Hot-pot

The traditional hot-pot has a funnel, in the centre of which charcoal is burned. The surrounding moat is filled with hot stock. A fondue pot, electric wok or chafing dish can be substituted. Each guest dips a piece of meat, fish or vegetable into the stock, retrieves it as soon as it is cooked, and then dips it in a hot sauce before eating it. At the end of the meal, any remaining vegetables are added to the simmering stock with cellophane noodles to serve as a soup. (Cellophane noodles are never eaten on their own. They absorb the flavour of the stock in soups and braised dishes.)

Dan Dan Noodles

This additional noodle dish may be served after the hot-pot, or you may simply add the cooked noodles with the sauce to the hot-pot broth making it a more substantial dish.

Chinese Hot-pot

Metric/Imperial

500 g/1 lb lamb fillet (or pork, beef or all three)
250 g/8 oz chicken breast meat, boned and skinned
250 g/8 oz peeled prawns (or fish fillet, or both)
250 g/8 oz fresh mushrooms
500 g/1 lb Chinese cabbage (or spinach)
2-3 cakes bean curd
250 g/8 oz cellophane (transparent) noodles
1.75 litres/3 pints clear stock (page 31)
Dip Sauce:
6 tablespoons soy sauce
2 teaspoons sugar
1 teaspoon sesame seed oil
3-4 spring onions, finely chopped
3 slices root ginger, peeled and finely chopped

Chinese hot-pot

1. Cut the meat and chicken into slices as thin as you possibly can; arrange them either separately on a large plate or together in small individual dishes.
2. Cut the prawns or fish into small slices also. Thinly slice the mushrooms and cut the cabbage or spinach and bean curd all into small pieces.
3. Soak the noodles until soft and arrange everything neatly, either together or separately in individual dishes.
4. Mix all the ingredients for the dip sauce together and pour into 4-6 little dishes. Place them on the table within easy reach of everyone.
5. Bring the stock or water to a fast boil and serve. (See introduction.)
6. When all the meats have been eaten, add all the vegetables to the pot, boil vigorously for a few minutes, then ladle out the contents into individual bowls, add the remaining dip sauce and serve as a most delicious soup to finish off the meal.

Variation:
Serve this delicious Sesame Hot Dip Sauce with the Chinese Hot-pot

6 tablespoons chopped spring onions
2 tablespoons chopped Chinese parsley
6 tablespoons soy sauce
6 tablespoons sesame seed paste
2 tablespoons rice wine or dry sherry
2 tablespoons sugar
2 tablespoons hot chilli or Tabasco sauce
2 tablespoons sesame seed oil
1 tablespoon salt

1. Mix together all the sauce ingredients and divide between individual bowls to allow each person to have his own sauce.

Dan Dan Noodles

Metric/Imperial
500 g/1 lb fresh noodles
900 ml/1 1/2 pints clear stock (see right)
Sauce:
2 tablespoons sesame seed paste
4 tablespoons water
4 tablespoons chopped spring onions
1 teaspoon garlic, peeled and crushed
1 tablespoon soy sauce
2 teaspoons red wine vinegar
2 teaspoons oil
1 teaspoon salt

1. Cook the noodles in plenty of boiled salted water until just tender. Bring the stock to the boil.
2. Make the sauce, mix the sesame seed paste with the water then add the remaining ingredients.
3. When the noodles are cooked, drain well. Divide the boiling stock between individual soup bowls, add the cooked noodles and top with the sauce. Each person tosses the contents of his bowl before eating.

Clear Stock

Metric/Imperial
1.5-1.75 kg/3-4 lb boiling chicken or pork spare ribs
2.75 litres/5 pints water
4-6 slices root ginger
3-4 spring onions

1. Place all the ingredients in a large saucepan – there is no need to peel the root ginger or cut the spring onions, as they are discarded after cooking. Bring to the boil, carefully skimming off any scum. Reduce the heat, cover and simmer very gently for about 2-2 1/2 hours.
2. Strain the stock when cool (after 2-3 hours), then refrigerate. The chicken carcass has given up its flavour to the stock during the long cooking and is not worth keeping.
3. Remove the solidified fat from the top of the stock before use. The stock will keep in the refrigerator for at least a week, after that boil it every 2 or 3 days.
Makes 2 litres/3 1/2 pints

Walnut Sweet

Metric/Imperial
250 g/8 oz shelled walnuts
175 g/6 oz jujubes or dates, stoned
oil for deep-frying
1.75 litres/3 pints water
275 g/10 oz granulated sugar
5 tablespoons cornflour, dissolved in 5 tablespoons water

1. Soak the walnuts in boiling water for 5 minutes, then remove the skins. Dry on absorbent kitchen paper.
2. Soak the jujubes in boiling water for 5 minutes, then drain and remove the stones.
3. Heat the oil to 180°C/350°F. Deep-fry the

walnuts until golden brown. (Walnuts burn easily, so remove them from the oil as soon as the colour changes.) Drain on absorbent kitchen paper until the excess oil has been removed.

4. Put the walnuts and dates in a blender and grind until very fine or rub through a sieve.

5. Bring the water to the boil in a saucepan. Stir in the sugar and the walnut mixture. When the sugar has dissolved, add the cornflour mixture and simmer, stirring continuously, until thickened. Serve hot.

Variation:

65 g/2½ oz rice powder or cornmeal may be used in place of the cornflour.

Almond Jelly with Chow Chow

Metric/Imperial

4 tablespoons gelatine
450 ml/¾ pint water
450 ml/¾ pint milk
1 tablespoon rice wine or sherry (optional)
3½ tablespoons sugar
1 teaspoon almond essence
1 large or 2 small cans chow chow (a preserve of ginger, fruit and orange peel)

1. Soften the gelatine in 125 ml/4 fl oz water then place in a heatproof bowl over a saucepan of hot water. Stir until dissolved.

2. Heat the remaining water with the milk, rice wine or sherry if using, sugar and almond essence, stirring until dissolved. Stir in the gelatine and mix well.

3. Pour the mixture into a lightly oiled rectangular pan and leave until cooled and set.

4. To serve, cut the almond jelly into triangular or rectangular bite-size pieces. Arrange in a large bowl and pour the chow chow into the centre. Chill before serving.

The day before:

Prepare the basic stock for the hot-pot and the clear stock for the Dan Dan noodles, if you intend serving them as a separate dish. Cool, cover and refrigerate both stocks.

On the day:

Slice the meats and fish for the hot-pot and prepare the vegetables. Cover and refrigerate. Make the dip sauces for the hot-pot. Make the Almond Jelly. Prepare the dates and deep-fry and grind the walnuts for the Walnut Sweet. Make the hot dip sauce for the Dan Dan Noodles.

To serve at 8.00 pm:

7.15: Turn out the jelly, cut it into pieces and arrange with the chow chow. Refrigerate.

7.30: Skim any fat off the soup stock, spoon it into the hot-pot and set the pot to heat. Make the Walnut Sweet and leave to simmer. Soak the cellophane noodles.

7.40: Arrange the accompaniments around the hot-pot with the drained cellophane noodles. Cook the fresh noodles for the Dan Dan noodle dish in boiling water; drain them thoroughly. Heat the clear stock, if necessary.

8.00: Serve the Chinese Hot-pot. At the end, add the cellophane noodles with any additional vegetables and serve as a soup, with the Dan Dan Noodles and sauce, if liked. Or serve the Dan Dan Noodles separately, with the clear stock and sauce.

Cook's Tip:

Cellophane Noodles. These transparent noodles are made from mung beans. They are sold in dried bundles from Chinese food stores and need to be soaked in warm water for 5 minutes before use. During this time they expand and become translucent. Cellophane noodles are usually added to soups or soup-type dishes.

Rice wine is also known as Shaoxing wine. It is made from glutinous rice. Sake or pale sherry are good substitutes.

M·E·N·U

· 8 ·

Grand Chinese Meal for 6

Chicken in Mustard Sauce
Shredded Fish with Celery

Cantonese Steamed Pork Spare Ribs
Fried Beef with Oyster Sauce
Quick-fried Spinach
Fried Crab with Black Beans

·

Sweet Peanut Cream
Deep-fried Sweet Potato Balls

Here is a more formal meal, from Canton in Southern China. Much of this province lies on the coast, so it is not surprising to find fish and shellfish on the menu. The Shredded Fish with Celery is a dish of great delicacy, which may be served hot or cold. In this instance, we've opted to serve it cold, as a starter with Chicken in Mustard Sauce. These dishes should be placed on the table before your guests arrive – Chinese etiquette demands that a guest is never invited to sit at an empty table.

The meal continues with steamed spare ribs and Fried Beef with Oyster Sauce, a regional favourite.

Oyster Sauce

Oyster sauce, shrimp sauce and shrimp paste are widely used in Chinese cooking, often in combination with meat. These sauces tend to be salty, so use them in moderation. The same rule applies to the salted black beans that are used in the crab dish. Soak them for 5 to 10 minutes before use and always use them in combination with other ingredients.

Chicken in Mustard Sauce

Metric/Imperial

1 pair of chicken breasts, boned and skinned
1/2 teaspoon salt
2 egg whites
1 tablespoon cornflour
150 ml/1/4 pint oil
Sauce:
2 tablespoons English mustard powder
1 tablespoon light soy sauce
1 tablespoon vinegar
2 teaspoons sesame seed oil

1. Mix the mustard powder with cold water to form a thin paste and let it mellow for 30 minutes before using. Thinly shred the chicken and mix with the salt, egg whites and cornflour.
2. Heat the oil in a wok, stir in the chicken over a medium heat. Separate the chicken shreds with chopsticks or a fork. As soon as their colour changes to pale white, scoop out with a slotted spoon and drain, then place on a serving dish.
3. Mix all the ingredients for the sauce together thoroughly and pour over the chicken. Serve cold.

Shredded Fish with Celery

Metric/Imperial

250 g/8 oz fish fillet (cod or haddock), skinned
1 teaspoon salt
1 tablespoon rice wine or dry sherry
1 egg white
1 tablespoon cornflour
1 celery heart
oil for deep-frying
25 g/1 oz cooked ham, thinly shredded, to garnish

1. Cut the fish into thin shreds. Place in a bowl and sprinkle with a pinch of the salt, then add first the wine or sherry, next the egg white and then the cornflour. Leave the fish to marinate.
2. Cut the celery heart into thin shreds.
3. Heat about 2 tablespoons of the oil in a wok, then stir-fry the celery with the remaining salt for about 1½ minutes. Place it on a serving dish.
4. Heat the remaining oil in a wok, reduce the heat to medium and deep-fry the fish shreds for about 2 minutes, separating them with a pair of chopsticks. When all the shreds are floating on the surface of the oil, scoop them out with a slotted spoon and drain, then place them on top of the celery.
5. Garnish with ham and serve either hot or cold.

Cantonese Steamed Pork Spare Ribs

Metric/Imperial

500 g/1 lb pork spare ribs
1 clove garlic, peeled and crushed
1 slice root ginger, peeled and finely chopped
1 tablespoon black bean sauce
1 tablespoon soy sauce
1 tablespoon rice wine or dry sherry
1 teaspoon sugar
1 teaspoon cornflour
To Garnish:
2 spring onions, cut into short lengths
1 small red pepper or chilli, thinly shredded

1. Chop the spare ribs into small pieces, mix with the garlic, root ginger, black bean sauce, soy sauce, wine or sherry, sugar and cornflour, then marinate for 15-20 minutes.
2. Place the spare ribs on a heatproof plate, put in a steamer and steam vigorously for 25-30 minutes. Garnish with spring onions and red pepper or chilli. Serve hot.

Deep-fried sweet potato balls; Sweet peanut cream

Fried Beef with Oyster Sauce

Metric/Imperial

1 tablespoon rice wine or dry sherry
1 tablespoon soy sauce
1 tablespoon cornflour
1/2 teaspoon sugar
1/2 teaspoon bicarbonate of soda
4 tablespoons water
freshly ground black pepper
6 tablespoons oil

500 g/1 lb lean beef fillet
2 spring onions, chopped
1 slice root ginger, peeled and chopped
2 tablespoons oyster sauce

1. Mix together the wine or sherry, soy sauce, cornflour, sugar, soda, water, pepper and 2 tablespoons of the oil in a bowl. Thinly slice the beef across the grain into bite-size pieces. Add to the sherry mixture and leave to marinate for at least 1 hour.
2. Heat the remaining oil in a wok. Add the beef and stir-fry for about 1½ minutes or until partially cooked. Remove with a slotted spoon.
3. Add half the spring onion, the root ginger and oyster sauce to the wok and stir-fry for 1 minute.
4. Add the beef and stir-fry for about 1 minute. Serve hot, garnished with the remaining spring onion. ·14·

Quick-fried Spinach

Metric/Imperial

3 tablespoons oil
2 tablespoons butter
1 teaspoon salt
3-4 garlic cloves, peeled and crushed
500 g/1 lb spinach
1 tablespoon soy sauce
1 teaspoon sugar
1 tablespoon rice wine or dry sherry

1. Heat the oil and butter in a large wok. When the butter has melted, add the salt and garlic. Stir and turn in the hot fat a few times.
2. Add the spinach and increase the heat to high. Stir and turn in the fat quickly until every leaf is well coated.
3. Sprinkle with the soy sauce, sugar and wine or sherry. Stir-fry for 1 minute over a high heat. Transfer to a hot serving dish and serve immediately.

Fried Crab with Black Beans

Metric/Imperial
1 large crab, boiled and cleaned
2 tablespoons oil
1 teaspoon root ginger, peeled and finely chopped
2 garlic cloves, peeled and crushed
2-3 spring onions, chopped
1½ tablespoons salted black beans, soaked for 10 minutes
*   and drained*
2 tablespoons rice wine or dry sherry
2 tablespoons soy sauce
1 tablespoon sugar
1 tablespoon cornflour, dissolved in 1 tablespoon water

1. Remove the legs from the crab and set aside. Extract the meat from the body and claws.
2. Heat the oil in a wok. Add the root ginger, garlic, spring onion and the black beans and stir-fry for 1 minute.
3. Add the crab meat, wine or sherry, soy sauce and sugar. Cover and cook for 10 minutes.
4. Add the cornflour mixture and cook, stirring, until thickened. Serve hot, garnished with the legs.

Sweet Peanut Cream

Metric/Imperial
50 g/2 oz smooth peanut butter
1 litre/1¾ pints milk or water
4 tablespoons sugar
4 teaspoons rice flour or cornflour, dissolved in
*   4 tablespoons water*

1. Put the peanut butter into a saucepan and gradually stir in the milk or water to make a paste.
2. Add the sugar and bring to the boil, stirring constantly. Add the dissolved rice flour or cornflour and cook, stirring, until the mixture thickens.

Deep-fried Sweet Potato Balls

Metric/Imperial
500 g/1 lb sweet potatoes
125 g/4 oz rice flour
50 g/2 oz demerara sugar
50 g/2 oz sesame seeds
oil for deep-frying

1. Put the potatoes in a saucepan, cover with water and bring to the boil. Reduce the heat and simmer for 15 to 20 minutes or until the potatoes are tender. Drain and peel. Mash the potatoes, then beat in the glutinous rice flour and sugar.
2. With damped hands, form the mixture into walnut-sized balls. Roll each ball in sesame seeds.
3. Heat the oil to 160°C/325°F. Deep-fry the potato balls until golden brown. Drain on absorbent kitchen paper. Serve hot as a dessert.

C · O · U · N · T · D · O · W · N

On the day:
Make and shape the Sweet Potato Balls. Cover lightly and chill until required. Make the Chicken in Mustard Sauce and Shredded Fish with Celery. Arrange on serving plates, cover and refrigerate. Slice and marinate the beef fillet. Boil the crab, if using, and extract the meat. Prepare the vegetables and garnishes.

To serve at 8.00 pm:
7.00: Marinate the pork spare ribs.
7.15: Fry the Sweet Potato Balls, drain and keep hot.
7.25: Make the Sweet Peanut Cream.
7.30: Put the spare ribs on to steam. Soak the salted black beans for the crab dish.
7.40: Make the Fried Crab with Black Beans.
7.50: Complete the crab and spare rib dishes.
8.00: Stir-fry the Beef with Oyster Sauce and the Quick-fried Spinach just before serving.

M·E·N·U

· 9 ·

Traditional Dinner for 6

Fish Slices in Hot Sauce
Jellied Chicken
Crystal-boiled Prawns in Jelly
·
Peking Roast Duck
Mandarin Pancakes
·
Walnut Sweet (page 31)
China Tea

The high point of this menu, Peking Roast Duck, is regarded as one of China's greatest dishes. In the area around Peking in Northern China, ducks are raised and fattened especially for this dish and special ovens fuelled with jujube wood are used for cooking. The skin is considered a particular delicacy and it is cut from the bird and served alongside the meat. Traditionally, Peking Duck is served with mandarin pancakes, spring onion flowers and hoisin sauce. The diner spreads a pancake with sauce, adds a few pieces of skin and meat, some spring onions and cucumber shreds, and then rolls up the pancake. Ready-made pancakes can be bought from Chinese food stores – they will keep in the refrigerator for two or three days. Steam them for 7 to 8 minutes before serving.

Choice of Wines

A meal such as this deserves good wines, and in China wines are considered so important that there is a special name given to dishes accompanied by them – they are called Ch'iu Tsai. Try Chinese rice wine, which is a rich golden colour and tastes a little like sherry.

Fish Slices in Hot Sauce

Metric/Imperial
500 g/1 lb fish fillet (cod or haddock), skinned
2 tablespoons rice wine or dry sherry
1 teaspoon salt
300 ml/½ pint oil
1 medium red pepper, cored, seeded and shredded
125 g/4 oz bamboo shoots, sliced
2-3 spring onions, cut into short lengths
2 slices root ginger, peeled and shredded
1 teaspoon sugar
125 ml/4 fl oz clear stock (page 31)
2 teaspoons chilli sauce

1. Cut the fish fillet into about 12 slices, marinate in the wine or sherry and ½ teaspoon of the salt for 10 minutes.
2. Heat the oil in a wok, add the fish slices piece by piece and fry for 2-3 minutes. Gently lift the fish out and drain on absorbent kitchen paper.
3. Pour off the excess oil, leaving about 1 tablespoon in the wok, add the red pepper, bamboo shoots, spring onions and root ginger. Stir a few times, then add the remaining salt, sugar and stock. Bring to the boil, add the fish and reduce to a low heat.
4. When the juice is almost all evaporated, add the chilli sauce and let it blend before carefully removing the fish slices to a serving dish. Allow to cool, then refrigerate until required.

Jellied Chicken

Metric/Imperial
1.5 kg/3-3½ lb roasting chicken
2 litres/3½ pints water
3 spring onions
3 slices root ginger
2 teaspoons salt
2 tablespoons rice wine or dry sherry

Crystal-boiled prawns in jelly; Jellied chicken; Fish slices in hot sauce

1. Boil the chicken in the water in a saucepan for about 1 hour. Remove the chicken, reserving the stock. Take the meat off the bone, skin and place the meat in a pudding basin.
2. Cover the meat with the cooking stock, add the spring onions, root ginger, salt and wine or sherry, plus the chicken skin.
3. Place the basin in a steamer or double saucepan and steam the chicken meat vigorously for at least 45 minutes. Remove the basin, discard the skin, spring onions and root ginger.
4. Place it in the refrigerator for 6-8 hours to set.
5. To serve, turn the basin on to a plate. The juice will have set as a delicious jelly.
6. The chicken bones can be used for making a stock in the remaining liquid. ·13·

Crystal-boiled Prawns in Jelly

Metric/Imperial
250 g/8 oz peeled prawns
300 ml/½ pint clear stock (page 31)
2 slices root ginger, peeled
1 spring onion
1 teaspoon Sichuan or black peppercorns
1 teaspoon salt
Jelly:
2 teaspoons gelatine
150 ml/¼ pint hot water
a few thin slices of cucumber, to garnish

1. Place the prawns in a saucepan with the stock, root ginger, spring onion, peppercorns and salt; bring to the boil, turn down the heat and simmer gently for about 5 minutes.
2. Take the prawns out and cut each one in half

lengthways. Arrange them in neat layers on a dish or in a jelly mould.
3. Strain the stock and discard the solid ingredients. Dissolve the gelatine in the hot water and add the strained stock.
4. Pour the gelatine over the prawns and leave to cool, then refrigerate until set.
5. To serve, turn the jelly out on to another dish and decorate the edge of the plate with thinly sliced cucumber pieces.

Peking Roast Duck

Metric/Imperial
1 × 2 kg/4½ lb duck
3 tablespoons honey or molasses
2 tablespoons red wine vinegar
2 tablespoons rice wine or dry sherry
250 ml/8 fl oz hot water
Accompaniments:
8-12 spring onion flowers
bean sauce or hoisin sauce
16 mandarin pancakes
1 cucumber, sliced
4 spring onions, shredded

1. Place the duck in a large saucepan and cover with boiling water. Boil for 5 minutes, then drain and cool under running water. Dry well.
2. Combine the honey or treacle, vinegar, wine or sherry and hot water. Brush the duck skin with this mixture. Brace the wings away from the body with two skewers. Hang the duck by the neck in a well-ventilated place to dry overnight.
3. Roast in a preheated oven (200°C/400°F), Gas Mark 6, for 30 minutes, then lower the oven temperature to (190°C/375°F), Gas Mark 5, and roast for a further 40 minutes or until the duck is tender.
4. To serve, cut off the crispy skin from the breast, sides and back of the duck and cut into 5 × 7.5 cm/

2 × 3 inch slices. Arrange these slices on a warmed serving dish.

5. Slice the meat from the breast and carcass and arrange on a separate serving dish, with the drumsticks and wings.

6. To eat: Each diner dips a spring onion brush in the bean sauce or hoisin sauce and brushes the sauce onto a mandarin pancake. He then places two pieces of cucumber and a little shredded spring onion in the centre of the pancake. This is topped with a slice of meat and a slice of duck skin. The pancake is then rolled up and eaten while still warm.

Mandarin Pancakes

Metric/Imperial
250 g/8 oz plain flour
250 ml/8 fl oz boiling water
2 tablespoons sesame seed oil

1. Sift the flour into a bowl. Add the boiling water, a little at a time, beating well with a wooden spoon after each addition. Knead the dough for 5 to 6 minutes, then cover and rest for 10 minutes.

2. Form the dough into a long roll, about 5 cm/2 inches in diameter. Cut the roll into 1 cm/½ inch slices. Roll into 15 cm/6 inch diameter pancakes.

3. Brush the tops of two pancakes with sesame seed oil and sandwich together, oiled sides facing inwards. Sandwich the remaining pancakes with the oil in the same way.

4. Heat a heavy, ungreased frying pan. Place a double-pancake in the pan and cook for 3 minutes on each side. (Brown spots will appear and some parts will start to bubble when the pancake is cooked.) Remove from the pan and cool slightly.

5. Pull the two pancakes apart and fold each one in half, oiled side inwards. Stack on a heatproof dish and keep hot while cooking the remaining pancakes.

6. When all the pancakes are cooked, place in a steamer and steam for 10 minutes.

On the day before:
Boil, then glaze the duck and leave to hang overnight.

On the day or night before:
Make Fish Slices in Hot Sauce, Jellied Chicken or Crystal-boiled Prawns in jelly, if using. Make and steam the Mandarin Pancakes and prepare the remaining accompaniments for the Peking Roast Duck, including the spring onion flowers (see Cook's Tip). Prepare the dates and walnuts for the dessert.

To serve at 8.00 pm:
6.25: Preheat the oven for the duck.
6.40: Place the duck in the oven.
7.10: Turn down the oven temperatures as directed. Turn out the Jellied Chicken and Crystal-boiled Prawns in Jelly and garnish.
7.45: Make the Walnut Sweet and keep warm over a very low heat.
7.50: Reheat the Mandarin Pancakes in a steamer. Slice the duck skin and place it on a serving dish. Arrange the sliced duck flesh on another dish with the drumsticks and wings. Keep warm.
8.00: Serve the cold hors d'oeuvres, followed by the Peking Roast Duck and its accompaniments.

Cook's Tip:
To make spring onion flowers, trim both ends of the stalk to about 7.5 cm/3 inches in length. Use a sharp knife to cut the green part downwards in strips to about one third of its length. Soak the onions in cold water for about an hour to curl the strips. They can be left in water for several hours. Drain and pat dry before use.

A delicious soup can be made from the duck carcass and could be served at the end of the meal. Simply boil the carcass in 1.2 litres/2 pints water for 30 minutes then remove the carcass. Add 750 g/1½ lb shredded Chinese cabbage, 1 diced cake of bean curd, 1 tablespoon soy sauce and 1 tablespoon wine vinegar. Boil for a further 10 minutes before serving.

M·E·N·U

· 10 ·

Formal Dinner for 4

Stewed Lamb
Fish in White Sauce
Pork with Mushrooms and Bean Sprouts
Shredded Duck Salad
Fried Rice

·

Jujube Cakes

This menu proves that you don't have to be wealthy to host a lavish Chinese meal. There are seven courses in this formal dinner, yet the quantities of the more expensive ingredients are so small as to be readily affordable. The emphasis is on variety of colour and texture. The ingredient used most lavishly is stewing lamb, the basis of a delectable dish which proves that not everything in China is stir-fried.

Sand-pot Stews

A Chinese stew is traditionally cooked over a slow charcoal fire. The utensil favoured for this is the clay sand-pot or Chinese casserole. It has a coarse, sand-textured beige exterior (often supported in a network of wire) and a brown, smoothly-glazed interior. The stew it produces is succulent, with meat of almost jelly-like tenderness.

Five Spice Powder

The tangy flavour of the stew comes from five spice powder, a mixture of star anise, fennel seeds, cloves, cinnamon and Sichuan peppercorns. It is highly pungent and should be used sparingly. It is sold at oriental food stores and keeps well in a sealed container.

Pork with mushrooms and bean sprouts; Fried rice

Stewed Lamb

Metric/Imperial
750 g/1 1/2 lb stewing lamb
1 garlic clove, peeled and crushed
2 slices root ginger, peeled
2 spring onions
2 tablespoons rice wine or dry sherry
1/2 teaspoon five-spice powder
3 tablespoons soy sauce
1 tablespoon sugar

1. Cut the lamb into matchbox-size pieces.
2. Place the cubes of lamb in a saucepan or flameproof casserole dish and add the garlic, root ginger, spring onions and wine or sherry, together with just enough water to cover. Bring it to the boil, then reduce the heat, cover and simmer for 1 hour.
3. Add the five-spice powder, soy sauce and sugar and cook for a further 30 minutes or until there is almost no juice left. Serve hot. ·6·

Fish in White Sauce

Metric/Imperial
1 egg white
1 teaspoon salt
1 tablespoon cornflour
500 g/1 lb plaice or sole fillets, cut into small pieces
3 tablespoons oil
2 spring onions, finely chopped
1 garlic clove, peeled and finely chopped
2 tablespoons rice wine or dry sherry
1 tablespoon water

1. Mix together the egg white, salt and 1 teaspoon of the cornflour. Add the fish and turn to coat. Heat the oil in a wok. Add the fish and fry gently until

golden. Remove with a slotted spoon.
2. Add the spring onions and garlic to the pan and stir-fry for 30 seconds. Return the fish slices to the wok with the wine or sherry.
3. Dissolve the remaining cornflour in the water and stir into the wok. Stir well so the sauce covers the fish and cook until the sauce thickens. Serve hot. ·11·

Pork with Mushrooms and Bean Sprouts

Metric/Imperial
250 g/8 oz pork fillet
2 tablespoons soy sauce
1 tablespoon cornflour
4 tablespoons oil
4 Chinese dried mushrooms, soaked in warm water for
*   20 minutes, squeezed dry, stemmed and quartered.*
*   Reserve the soaking liquid.*
250 g/8 oz bean sprouts
1 red pepper, cored, seeded and sliced
125 g/4 oz mangetout
125 g/4 oz Chinese cabbage, shredded
1 1/2 teaspoons salt
2 tablespoons rice wine or dry sherry
lime rind, to garnish

1. Cut the pork into thin slices about the size of a large postage stamp. Mix together the soy sauce and the cornflour, then add the pork.
2. Heat about half the oil in a wok and stir-fry the pork slices for about 1 minute or until lightly coloured. Remove the pork with a slotted spoon.
3. Heat the remaining oil, stir-fry the mushrooms, bean sprouts, pepper, mangetout and Chinese cabbage. Add the salt, pork, and rice wine or sherry, stirring well. Cook for a further minute or so, stirring constantly and, if necessary, add a little of the reserved soaking liquid. Serve hot garnished with lime rind. ·12·

Shredded Duck Salad

Metric/Imperial
2 tablespoons red wine vinegar
2 tablespoons sugar
2 tablespoons sesame seed oil
2 tablespoons soy sauce
1 teaspoon made mustard
1/2 teaspoon salt
125 g/4 oz carrots, shredded
125 g/4 oz cucumber, peeled and shredded
75 g/3 oz cabbage or Chinese cabbage, cored and shredded
500 g/1 lb roast duck or chicken meat, shredded

1. Combine the vinegar, sugar, sesame seed oil, soy sauce, mustard and salt in a bowl; mix thoroughly.
2. Arrange the vegetables on a serving plate. Put the shredded duck or chicken on top. Pour over the dressing just before serving. ·8·9·

Fried Rice

Metric/Imperial
2 spring onions, finely chopped
3 eggs
1 teaspoon salt
4 tablespoons oil
50 g/2 oz cooked ham or Cha Shao pork, diced
50 g/2 oz cooked prawns, peeled
125 g/4 oz green peas
175 g/6 oz long-grain rice, cooked
1 1/2 tablespoons soy sauce

1. Mix half of the spring onions with the eggs, add a pinch of salt and beat lightly.
2. Heat a third of the oil in a wok, then add the eggs and stir until scrambled. When the eggs sets, transfer them to a preheated plate and break them into small pieces with a fork.
3. Heat another third of the oil in the wok. Add the meat cubes, the prawns, peas and the remaining salt to the wok and stir-fry for about 1 minute then remove with a slotted spoon and set aside.
4. Heat the remaining oil in the wok, then add the spring onions and cooked rice. Stir to separate each grain of rice. Add the soy sauce and stir until it is evenly blended with the rice, then add the eggs, ham or pork, prawns and peas. Reduce the heat. Serve as soon as everything is well mixed. ·1·13·

Jujube Cakes

Metric/Imperial
250 g/8 oz jujubes or dates
250 g/8 oz glutinous rice flour

1. Put the jujubes in a pan, cover with cold water and bring to the boil. Simmer for 1 hour or until soft. Drain, then remove the skins and stones. If using dates, remove the stones and heat to soften.
2. Beat the fruit to form a paste. Add the rice flour and knead to make a soft dough. Roll out to 5 mm/ 1/4 inch thick and cut out small shapes, using fancy cutters. Steam the cakes for 5 minutes.

C · O · U · N · T · D · O · W · N

On the day:
Prepare the meats, fish, vegetables, garnishes and Duck Salad. Refrigerate. Mix the dressing for the salad. Make the Jujube Cakes. Cook the rice.

To serve at 8.00 pm:
6.30: Prepare the Stewed Lamb.
7.15: Soak the dried mushrooms for the pork dish.
7.30: Add the spice, soy sauce and sugar to the lamb and continue cooking. Heat the stock for the soup. Scramble the eggs and cook the ham, prawns and peas for the Fried Rice. Set aside. Coat the fish slices.
7.45: Prepare the Fish in White Sauce and stir-fry the Pork with Mushrooms and Bean Sprouts.
7.55: Finish the Fried Rice. Dress the Duck Salad.
8.00: Steam the Jujube Cakes while eating the savoury course.

M·E·N·U

· 11 ·

Sichuan Meal for 4

Prawns in Tomato Sauce
Braised Fish in Chilli Sauce
Chinese Cabbage Casserole
Chinese Mushroom Soup

·

Sesame Seed Biscuits

Sichuan or Szechuan is one of the most prosperous regions of China and its hearty, highly spiced food is well known in the West. Probably their most famous culinary export is Sichuan peppercorns, which now appear on menus the world over. These are much stronger and more fragrant than either black or white peppercorns, so treat them with respect.

This menu is strongly representative of the region, and also utilizes chilli sauce and chilli bean paste, two more ingredients to fire your guests with enthusiasm!

Dry-Frying

This is a cooking method unique to Sichuan. The principal ingredients are slowly stir-fried until they are almost dry, then moistened with sauces and wine and finished at high heat with additional flavourings.

Preserving Techniques

This region is also known for its preserving techniques, including salting, drying, smoking and pickling. Pickles are often served at a Sichuan meal and feature on this menu. Pungent vegetables like garlic and spring onions are also used extensively. Peanuts, sesame seeds, cashews, walnuts and pine nuts are also valued for their aromatic flavours.

Prawns in Tomato Sauce

Metric/Imperial

1 teaspoon salt
250 g/8 oz peeled raw prawns
1 egg white
2 teaspoons cornflour
oil for deep-frying
1 spring onion, finely chopped
2 slices root ginger, peeled and finely chopped
1 clove garlic, peeled and finely chopped
1 tablespoon rice wine or dry sherry
1 tablespoon tomato paste
1 tablespoon chilli sauce
1 lettuce heart

1. Mix a pinch of the salt with the prawns, add the egg white, then the cornflour.
2. Heat the oil in a wok, add the prawns, stirring to separate, and deep-fry for about 30 seconds over a medium heat. Remove with a slotted spoon and drain.
3. Pour off the excess oil, leaving about 1 tablespoon in the wok, turn the heat up to high, add the spring onion, root ginger and garlic to flavour the oil, then add the prawns and stir-fry for 1-2 minutes.
4. Add the remaining salt, wine or sherry, tomato paste and chilli sauce, stirring continually. When all the sauces are well blended, remove and serve on a bed of lettuce leaves.

Braised Fish in Chilli Sauce

Metric/Imperial

1 × 750 g/1½ lb fish (sea bass, carp, grey mullet or
*   trout)*
oil for deep-frying
2 slices root ginger, peeled and finely chopped
1 clove garlic, peeled and finely chopped
2 tablespoons chilli bean paste
1 tablespoon soy sauce
2 tablespoons rice wine or dry sherry
½ teaspoon salt
3 tablespoons clear stock (page 31)
1 teaspoon sugar
2 teaspoons vinegar
1 teaspoon chilli sauce
2 teaspoons cornflour mixed with 1 tablespoon water
2 spring onions, finely chopped, to garnish

1. Scale and clean the fish. Slash both sides of the fish diagonally as deep as the bone at intervals of about 2 cm (¾ inch).
2. Heat the oil in a wok until hot and deep-fry the fish for about 5 minutes, turning it over once. Remove the fish with a slotted spoon.
3. Pour off the excess oil, leaving about 1 tablespoon in the wok, add the root ginger, garlic, chilli bean paste, soy sauce and wine or sherry, stirring until smooth, then return the fish to the wok, together with the salt and stock. Reduce the heat and simmer for 2-3 minutes, then turn the fish over, and add the sugar, vinegar, chilli sauce and cornflour mixture. Increase the heat to high to thicken the sauce. Garnish with finely chopped spring onions and serve hot. ·8·10·

Cook's Tip:
The amount of chilli bean paste and chilli sauce can either be increased or reduced according to how hot you like your food. If you have difficulty in finding chilli bean paste, substitute with crushed yellow bean sauce mixed with chilli sauce.

Chinese Cabbage Casserole

Metric/Imperial

750 g/1½-1¾ lb Chinese cabbage
3-4 Chinese dried mushrooms, soaked in warm water for
*   10 minutes, squeezed dry and stemmed. Reserve the*
*   soaking liquid*
1 tablespoon dried shrimps (see Cook's Tip)
500 g/1 lb bamboo shoots or carrots

Chinese cabbage casserole; Braised fish in chilli sauce

50 g/2 oz cooked ham
300 ml/½ pint clear stock (page 31)
1 teaspoon salt
1 tablespoon rice wine or dry sherry

1. Discard the tough, outer cabbage leaves, trim off the hard root, then cut the cabbage into 3-4 sections depending on its length. Place the sections on the bottom of a casserole or Chinese sand-pot (or saucepan).
2. Place the mushrooms and the shrimps on top of the cabbage sections.
3. Cut the bamboo shoots or carrots into thin slices and place them on top with the cabbage, mushrooms and shrimps.
4. Cut the ham into thin slices also and add to the pot.

5. Finally add the stock together with the reserved water to the pot. The level of liquid should be not too near the top as a lot of water will come out of the cabbage during cooking. Now add the salt and cook gently for 30 minutes over a moderate heat, stirring occasionally.
6. Just before serving, add the wine or sherry, bring to the boil and serve hot with Pickled Cucumber. ·2·

Cook's Tip:
Dried shrimps are an acquired taste. They come in different sizes and have been salted and dried in the sun. They should be soaked in warm water for at least 30 minutes, then drained and rinsed before use. They will keep in the dry state in an air-tight container.

47

Chinese Mushroom Soup

Metric/Imperial

125 g/4 oz fresh mushrooms (preferably black field
   mushrooms)
2 teaspoons cornflour
1 tablespoon cold water
3 egg whites
2 teaspoons salt
600 ml/1 pint clear stock (page 31)
1 teaspoon finely chopped spring onion, to garnish

1. Wash and slice the mushrooms.
2. Mix the cornflour with the water. Stir the egg whites with your fingers to loosen them (do not use a whisk as too much air will make them frothy) and add a pinch of the salt.
3. Bring the stock to the boil and add the mushrooms. Boil together for 1 minute, then add the cornflour mixture, stirring constantly.
4. Add the remaining salt and pour the egg white very slowly into the soup, stirring all the time.
5. Garnish with the spring onions and serve hot.

Sesame Seed Biscuits

Metric/Imperial

250 g/8 oz self-raising flour, sifted
25 g/1 oz sugar
2 tablespoons sesame seeds
15 g/½ oz lard
4 tablespoons water
oil for deep-frying

1. Mix together the flour, sugar, sesame seeds, lard and water and knead well to form a soft dough.
2. Place the dough on a floured surface and roll out to a 3 mm/¼ inch thickness. Cut into 1.5 × 5 cm/ ¾ × 2 inch rectangles and make a slit in the centre of each. Bring one end of the rectangle through the slit to form a twist.

3. Heat the oil to 160°C/325°F. Deep-fry the biscuits until golden brown. Drain on absorbent kitchen paper and serve either hot or cold.

C · O · U · N · T · D · O · W · N

On the day:
Prepare the meat, fish, vegetables and garnishes including soaking the dried shrimps for the Chinese Cabbage Casserole. In another bowl, soak the mushrooms for both the casserole and the soup. Cover and refrigerate. Prepare the pickled cucumber (see Cook's tip) and make the biscuits. Make the stock, for the soup, if necessary.

To serve at 8.00 pm:
7.20: Assemble the Chinese Cabbage Casserole, using 4 of the reconstituted mushrooms, and leave to cook. Deep-fry the prawns for Prawns in Tomato Sauce, and set aside.
7.30: Deep-fry the fish for the Braised Fish in Chilli Sauce, if using, and set aside. Put the stock on for the soup.
7.40: Prepare the remaining mushrooms and add them to the soup with the remaining ingredients. Keep warm over a low heat.
7.50: Finish the braised fish dish. Complete the Prawns in Tomato Sauce. Add the wine or sherry to the cabbage casserole and bring it to the boil.
8.00: Transfer the dishes to serving plates, garnish and serve.

Cook's Tip:
Pickled Cucumber: To prepare pickled cucumber simply bring 2 tablespoons vinegar, 1 tablespoon brown sugar and 1 teaspoon ground ginger to the boil. Pour this over 1 thinly sliced cucumber and leave until cold. Stir in 1 teaspoon sesame seed oil just before serving.

Deep-frying: A wok or deep-fryer can be used for this method. The food is normally dipped into a batter of some sort before frying in hot oil. It is advisable to use a fat thermometer to check the temperature of the oil.

M·E·N·U

· 12 ·

Celebration Dinner for 6

Barbecued Pork
Bean Sprouts with Beef
Stir-fried Chicken Livers with Prawns and Broccoli
Steamed Sweet and Sour Fish
Stir-fried Lettuce
Fried Rice (page 44)
Chicken and Ham Soup

·

Gingered Fruit
China Tea

If you don't have an occasion to celebrate right now, invent one, for this menu is well worth trying. The featured main course dishes should be served simultaneously, for their complementary colours make a dramatic display. For maximum effect, serve them on black plates set on a white cloth, or vice versa. The steamed whole fish looks spectacular with its sweet and sour sauce. Choose trout, carp, mullet or salmon and slash the skin several times before cooking.

Using Ginger

One of the ingredients of the Steamed Sweet and Sour fish and others on this menu is ginger, which is an important Chinese flavouring. Sold by weight, root ginger should be peeled and sliced or shredded before use. A piece of root ginger will keep for weeks in a cool, dry place. Alternatively, store grated or shredded ginger submerged in a jar of sherry or oil. To extract the ginger juice (as used in the Barbecued Pork), squeeze peeled ginger in a garlic crusher.

Barbecued Pork

Metric/Imperial

2 tablespoons soy sauce
2 tablespoons rice wine or dry sherry
2 teaspoons sesame seed oil
1 teaspoon salt
2 teaspoons ginger juice
2 tablespoons clear honey or corn syrup
50 g/2 oz sugar
1-2 cloves garlic, peeled and minced
1 kg/2 lb pork shoulder, cut into 5 × 5 × 10 cm/2 × 2
*   × 4 inch pieces*

1. Mix together the soy sauce, wine or sherry, oil, salt, ginger, honey or syrup, sugar and garlic in a dish. Add the pork and leave to marinate for at least 6 hours in the refrigerator, turning the meat occasionally.

2. Place the pork on a wire rack in a roasting pan. Roast in a preheated moderate oven (180°C/350°F) Gas Mark 4, for 40 to 45 minutes or until tender, basting with the pan juices frequently.

3. Cut into serving pieces and arrange on a plate. Serve hot or cold. ·13·

Bean Sprouts with Beef

Metric/Imperial

500 g/1 lb minced beef
1 tablespoon rice wine or dry sherry
1 tablespoon soy sauce
1 teaspoon cornflour
2 tablespoons oil
2 spring onions, chopped
500 g/1 lb bean sprouts
1 teaspoon salt
250 ml/8 fl oz water

1. Mix the beef with the wine or sherry, soy sauce and cornflour. Cover and refrigerate for 20 minutes. Heat the oil in a wok.
2. Add the meat mixture and stir-fry until the beef is well browned. Add the spring onions, bean sprouts and salt and stir-fry over a high heat for approximately 1 minute.
3. Add the water. Bring to the boil, cover and cook for 15 minutes or until the meat and bean sprouts are tender. Serve hot. ·5·

Stir-fried Chicken Livers with Prawns and Broccoli

Metric/Imperial
350 g/12 oz broccoli, broken into small florets
250 g/8 oz shelled prawns, de-veined
1 teaspoon salt
4 tablespoons oil
250 g/8 oz chicken livers
1½ tablespoons soy sauce
2 slices root ginger, peeled and shredded
1 teaspoon sugar
2 tablespoons rice wine or dry sherry

1. Parboil the broccoli florets for 3 minutes, then drain well.
2. Sprinkle the prawns with the salt and 1 tablespoon of the oil. Cut each liver into four pieces. Sprinkle with half the soy sauce and another 1 tablespoon of the oil.
3. Heat the remaining oil in a wok over a high heat. Add the root ginger and stir-fry for 20 seconds. Add the prawns and chicken livers and stir-fry for 1-2 minutes. Add the broccoli florets, sugar and wine or sherry.
4 Bring to the boil. Sprinkle with remaining soy sauce. Stir-fry for 2 minutes. Serve hot.

Bean sprouts with beef; Barbecued pork

Steamed Sweet and Sour Fish

Metric/Imperial
750 g/1½ lb whole fish (trout, carp, mullet, salmon, etc.), cleaned
2 teaspoons salt
1½ tablespoons oil
3 tablespoons lard
2 small chilli peppers, seeded and shredded
6 onions, cut into 2 inch pieces
6 slices root ginger, shredded
1 red pepper, cored, seeded and shredded
3 pieces canned bamboo shoot, shredded
3 tablespoons soy sauce
3 tablespoons wine vinegar
1½ tablespoons sugar
1½ tablespoons tomato purée
3 tablespoons orange juice
1 tablespoon cornflour dissolved in
    5 tablespoons chicken stock

1. With a sharp knife, score the fish on both sides with diagonal parallel cuts. Rub the fish inside and out with the salt and oil and leave for 30 minutes.
2. Place the fish on an oval heatproof serving dish and put the dish in a steamer. Steam vigorously for 15 minutes.
3. Melt the lard in a wok over moderate heat. Add the chilli peppers and stir-fry for 1 minute. Add all the remaining ingredients, except the cornflour paste, and stir-fry for a further 15 seconds.
4. Add the cornflour mixture and stir until the sauce thickens. Garnish the fish with the solid ingredients from the pan and carefully pour the sauce over the fish. Serve hot.
Cook's Tip:
It is vital that you buy fish that is really fresh. Look for clear, full eyes (not sunken), bright-red gills, firm skin and shiny, slightly soft scales.

Stir-fried Lettuce

Metric/Imperial

1 large cos lettuce
2-3 tablespoons oil
1 teaspoon salt
1 teaspoon sugar

1. Discard the tough outer leaves and wash the lettuce well. Tear the larger leaves into 2 or 3 pieces, shaking off the excess water.
2. Heat the oil in a wok, add the salt followed by the lettuce leaves and stir vigorously as though tossing a salad. Add the sugar and continue stirring. As soon as the leaves become slightly limp quickly transfer them to a serving dish and serve. ·2·8·14·

Chicken and Ham Soup

Metric/Imperial

125 g/4 oz chicken breast meat, skinned and boned
125 g/4 oz cooked ham
600 ml/1 pint clear stock (page 31)
1 teaspoon finely chopped spring onion, to garnish
1 teaspoon salt

1. Thinly slice the chicken and ham and cut into small pieces.
2. Bring the stock to the boil, add the chicken and ham slices. Cook for 1 minute.
3. Place the spring onions and salt in a serving bowl, pour in the soup and serve hot.

Cook's Tip:
The Chinese traditionally make marvellous soups merely by stir-frying a handful of fresh greens or whatever is at hand, adding some water and seasoning and bringing to a rapid boil. If you have some ready-made stock, there is no limit to what you can make into an instantly prepared soup. In China the very best stock is made from a whole chicken, a whole duck or a leg of ham or pork.

Gingered Fruit

Metric/Imperial

1 × 425 g/15 oz can pineapple pieces, drained or
  1 large fresh pineapple, skinned, cored and roughly
  chopped
1 × 300 g/11 oz can lychees, drained
1 tablespoon chopped glacé cherries
2 tablespoons chopped crystallized ginger
25 g/1 oz flaked, toasted almonds

1. Mix together the pineapple, lychees, cherries and ginger in a mixing bowl. Cover and chill well in the refrigerator for about 1 hour.
2. Sprinkle the almonds over the top and serve immediately in small bowls.

C · O · U · N · T · D · O · W · N

On the day:
Prepare the meat, fish, vegetables and garnishes. Cover and refrigerate. Marinate the pork. Boil the rice for Fried Rice. Make the stock for the soup if required. Prepare the Gingered Fruits. Cover and place in the refrigerator.

To serve at 8.00 pm:
6.45: Preheat the oven for the pork.
7.00: Prepare the beef. Cover and refrigerate. Salt the fish. Place the pork in the oven.
7.15: Baste the pork.
7.30: Begin cooking the Bean Sprouts with Beef and leave to cook. Baste pork.
7.40: Heat the stock for the soup. Put the fish to steam and make the sauce, set aside. Scramble the eggs and cook the ham, prawns and peas.
7.45: Slice the pork and keep hot.
7.50: Complete the Fried Rice and stir-fry the Chicken Livers with Prawns and Broccoli. Cook the Stir-fried Lettuce. Heat the sauce and complete the soup.
8.00: Transfer the dishes to serving plates, garnish and serve immediately.

M·E·N·U

· 13 ·

Birthday Meal for 4

Sichuan Bang-Bang Chicken or
Soya Duck
Fried Prawns with Beans
Cha Shao Quick Roast Pork
Boiled Noodles
Sliced Fish Soup

·

Fresh Fruit

As a birthday treat, this menu stars Cha Shao roast pork. In China, roasting is a little-used culinary technique, as many homes do not have an oven. Restauranteurs, especially those in Peking and Canton, delight in offering roast meat, and specialise in Cha Shao, a method of quick roasting at high temperatures. The meat, which must be a very tender cut, is marinaded before cooking, and the high heat leads to the formation of a crisp, honeyed outer layer enclosing a juicy, tender interior.

A Symbol of Long Life

Noodles are always served at birthday celebrations, since the Chinese regard them as symbols of long life. Boiled noodles may not sound very appetizing, but this dish is a mouthwatering medley and includes stir-fried vegetables and ginger, served with a soya-based sauce.

Extra Guests

For a more formal birthday dinner, simply serve the Bang-Bang Chicken or Soya Duck as cold hors d'oeuvres and add some extra dishes such as Steamed Beef and Spinach Salad (see pages 59 and 60).

Sichuan Bang-Bang Chicken

Metric/Imperial

175 g/6 oz chicken breast meat, boned and skinned
1 lettuce heart
Sauce:
1 tablespoon sesame seed paste
1 tablespoon light soy sauce
2 teaspoons vinegar
1 teaspoon chilli sauce
1 teaspoon sugar
2 tablespoons clear stock (page 31)

1. Cover the chicken meat with cold water in a saucepan and bring to the boil, then reduce the heat and simmer gently for 10 minutes. Remove the chicken and beat it with a rolling pin until soft – hence the name of the dish.
2. Cut the lettuce leaves into shreds and place them on a serving dish. Pull the chicken meat into shreds with your fingers and place on top of the lettuce leaves.
3. Mix together all the ingredients for the sauce and pour evenly over the chicken until covered. Serve when cold. ·8·

Soya Duck

Metric/Imperial

1 × 2 kg/4½-4¾ lb duckling, cleaned
1.2 litres/2 pints water
2 teaspoons salt
4 spring onions
4 slices root ginger
1 teaspoon five-spice powder
3 tablespoons rice wine or dry sherry
6 tablespoons dark soy sauce
125 g/4 oz demerara sugar
1 tablespoon sesame seed oil

1. Bring the water to the boil in a large saucepan, blanch the duck for 1 minute, then dry it thoroughly both inside and out. Rub a little salt inside it.
2. Add the remaining salt, spring onions, root ginger and five-spice powder and bring to the boil.
3. Return the duck to the pot and add the wine or sherry, soy sauce and sugar. Cover and simmer gently for 1½ hours, then lift the duck out and rub it all over with sesame seed oil.
4. Boil the cooking liquid uncovered, then use it to baste the duck several times before chopping the meat into small pieces. Serve hot or cold. ·9·

Fried Prawns with Beans

Metric/Imperial

150 g/5 oz broad beans
3½ teaspoons rice wine or dry sherry
2½ teaspoons salt
freshly ground black pepper
1 small egg white
2 teaspoons cornflour
500 g/1 lb raw prawns, shelled and deveined
½ teaspoon sugar
1 tablespoon water
2 tablespoons oil
1 small spring onion, chopped

1. Cook the beans in boiling water until tender.
2. Mix together 1 tablespoon of the wine or sherry, 1 teaspoon of the salt, the pepper, egg white and 1 teaspoon of the cornflour in a bowl. Add the prawns and leave to marinate for 30 minutes.
3. Mix together the remaining wine or sherry, salt and cornflour with the sugar and water.
4. Heat the oil in a wok. Add the prawns and stir-fry for about 1½ minutes. Transfer to a serving dish and keep warm, loosely covered.
5. Add the beans and spring onion to the wok and stir-fry for a few seconds. Add the sugar mixture. Simmer until thickened. Add to the prawns.

Cha Shao Quick Roast Pork

Metric/Imperial
1 kg/2 lb pork fillet or tenderloin
Marinade:
1½ tablespoons soy sauce
1½ teaspoons red bean curd
1½ tablespoons rice wine or dry sherry
1 tablespoon sweet bean sauce or hoisin sauce
½ teaspoon salt
½ teaspoon pepper
1 tablespoon water
1½ teaspoons sugar or honey
1 tablespoon oil

1. Place the pork fillet in a shallow dish. Combine the marinade ingredients and pour over the pork. Turn the meat in the marinade until well coated. Leave for 2 hours, turning every 20 minutes.
2. Put the pork on a wire rack in a roasting pan and place in the top of a preheated hot oven (220°C/425°F) Gas Mark 7. Roast for 12 minutes.
3. Remove the pork from the oven and cut across the grain into 5 mm/¼ inch thick slices.

Cook's Tip:
Meat is normally either sliced or shredded. It should be cut across the grain to help tenderise it.

Bean Sauce is available in yellow and black varieties. It is made from soy beans and sold in cans.

Soya duck; Sichuan bang-bang chicken

Boiled Noodles

Metric/Imperial

250 g/8 oz fresh mushrooms
250 g/8 oz chicken meat, cut into matchstick strips
2 teaspoons cornflour
300 g/11 oz egg noodles
1 litre/1¾ pints clear stock (page 31)
8 tablespoons oil
250 g/8 oz bamboo shoots, cut into fine strips
250 g/8 oz spinach leaves, torn into fine strips
4 spring onions, finely chopped
2 slices root ginger, peeled and finely chopped
Sauce:
8 tablespoons soy sauce
4 tablespoons rice wine or dry sherry
2 teaspoons salt
2 teaspoons sugar

1. Thinly slice the mushrooms. Toss the chicken strips in the cornflour.
2. Bring a saucepan of water to the boil, add the noodles and simmer for 5 minutes until soft but not sticky. Drain and place in a large preheated bowl, keep warm.
3. Bring the stock to the boil and then pour it over the cooked noodles.
4. Heat the oil in a wok and add the chicken, bamboo shoots, mushrooms, spinach, spring onions and root ginger. Stir-fry for about 1 minute.
5. Mix together the sauce ingredients and pour into the wok. Continue stirring for another 1 to 2 minutes. Pour the mixture over the noodles and the stock and serve. ·1·10·

Sliced Fish Soup

Metric/Imperial

250 g/8 oz fish fillet (plaice or sole), skinned
1 egg white
1 tablespoon cornflour

1 lettuce heart
600 ml/1 pint clear stock (page 31)
salt
freshly ground white pepper
1 teaspoon finely chopped spring onion, to garnish

1. Cut the fish fillet into large slices about the size of a matchbox, mix with the egg white and cornflour. Thinly shred the lettuce heart.
2. Bring the stock to the boil, add the salt and fish slices. Simmer for 1 minute.
3. Place the shredded lettuce in a large serving bowl, add plenty of white pepper and pour the soup over it. Garnish with spring onions and serve hot. ·6·

C · O · U · N · T · D · O · W · N

On the day:
Prepare the meat, vegetables and garnishes. Marinate the pork, turning it frequently. Make the Bang-Bang Chicken, pouring the sauce over it when cold or prepare the duck. Garnish, cover and refrigerate. Make the stock for the soup, if necessary.

To serve at 8.00 pm:
6.00: Prepare the duck and leave to simmer.
6.15: Blanch the broad beans and leave the prawns to marinate. Mix together the remaining ingredients for the broad bean dish and set aside.
7.30: Preheat the oven for the roast pork. Remove the duck to a rack, rub with sesame seed oil. Reduce the sauce and baste the duck several times before serving. Cook the noodles.
7.40: Roast the pork. Put the stock for the soup on to boil and mix the fish with egg white and cornflour. Stir-fry the additional ingredients for the noodle dish and make the sauce.
7.50: Chop the duck meat. Slice the pork. Stir-fry the prawns with beans.
7.55: Finish the soup and the noodles.
8.00: Transfer all food to serving plates, garnish and serve immediately. The Bang-Bang Chicken may be served as a starter, or it may accompany the meal.

M·E·N·U

· 14 ·

Casual Dinner for 4

Fried Fish Slices
Chicken with Cashew Nuts
Steamed Beef Sichuan-style
Spring Rolls
Spinach Salad
Plain Boiled Rice (page 12)
Pork, Ham and Bamboo Shoot Soup

This meal would provide the ideal introduction to Chinese food for guests wary of anything not Western. The recipes have been culled from all over China, so give an inkling of the variety of dishes available, with the emphasis on delicate rather than highly spiced flavours.

Spring Rolls

The menu includes that all-time favourite, the spring roll, top of the takeaway list but even more delicious when freshly made at home. The spring roll consists of a deep-fried crisp pancake enclosing a tasty mixture of meat, poultry or shellfish and lightly cooked vegetables. You can buy frozen spring roll wrappers but it is easy to make your own, following the simple recipe in this menu. Professional Chinese cooks make a more elaborate dough. It has the consistency of marshmallow and they use a heavy pan to press it to paper thin sheets.

Sesame Seed Oil

Simplicity is the key to the spinach salad, which owes its excellence to the dressing. It is important to use sesame seed oil, which is much favoured in Chinese cooking. It is now widely used in China.

Fried Fish Slices

Metric/Imperial

500 g/1 lb fish fillet (plaice or sole), skinned
1 tablespoon rice wine or dry sherry
1 egg white
1 tablespoon cornflour
300 ml/½ pint oil
1 garlic clove, peeled and chopped
1 spring onion, chopped
1 slice root ginger, peeled and shredded
¼ red pepper, cored and sliced
Sauce:
150 ml/4 fl oz clear stock (page 31)
2 teaspoons salt
1 teaspoon sugar
2 teaspoons cornflour
1 teaspoon sesame seed oil

1. Cut the fish into thin 5 cm/2 inch slices. Mix together the wine or sherry, egg white and cornflour, then marinate the fish in it for about 20 minutes.
2. Heat the oil in a wok until hot, then fry the fish for 2 to 3 minutes. Remove and drain the fish retaining about 1 tablespoon oil. Add the garlic, spring onion, root ginger and red pepper.
3. Blend together the sauce ingredients, add to the wok with the fish, stir over the heat and serve. ·11·

Chicken with Cashew Nuts

Metric/Imperial

1 egg white
2 tablespoons rice wine or dry sherry
1 teaspoon salt
pinch of pepper
1 teaspoon cornflour
1 chicken breast, skinned, boned and cut into slices
9 tablespoons oil
125 g/4 oz cashew nuts
1 spring onion, chopped
1 green pepper, cored, seeded and cut into pieces
150 g/6 oz canned bamboo shoot, sliced
1 tablespoon soy sauce
1 teaspoon sugar
1 teaspoon cornflour, dissolved in 1 tablespoon water

Pork, ham and bamboo shoot soup

1. Mix together the egg white, 1 tablespoon of the wine or sherry, the salt, pepper and cornflour. Add the chicken and turn to coat with the mixture. Heat 3 tablespoons of the oil in a pan. Add the chicken and stir-fry until golden. Remove from the heat.

2. Heat 5 tablespoons of the remaining oil in a wok. Add the cashew nuts and fry until lightly browned. Remove with a slotted spoon and drain on absorbent kitchen paper.

3. Heat the remaining oil in the wok. Add the spring onion, green pepper and bamboo shoot and stir-fry for 1 minute.

4. Add the remaining wine or sherry, the soy sauce, sugar and cornflour mixture and cook, stirring, until thickened. Add the chicken, turn to coat in the sauce and heat through. Serve hot, sprinkled with cashew nuts. ·3·6·

Steamed Beef Sichuan-style

Metric/Imperial
750 g/1 ½ lb beef (topside)
1 teaspoon salt
2 tablespoons rice wine or dry sherry
1 tablespoon soy sauce
2 tablespoons chilli bean paste
1 teaspoon sugar
3 slices root ginger, peeled and finely chopped
4 spring onions, finely chopped
freshly ground Sichuan or black pepper
1 tablespoon oil
75 g/3 oz ground rice
1 lettuce or cabbage
To garnish:
1 teaspoon sesame seed oil
finely chopped spring onion

1. Cut the beef into matchbox-size thin slices, combine the salt, wine or sherry, soy sauce, chilli bean paste, sugar, root ginger, spring onions, pepper and oil in a bowl. Add the beef, cover and refrigerate. Leave to marinate for at least 20 minutes, preferably overnight.

2. Meanwhile, roast the ground rice in a dry frying pan, until it is aromatic and a light golden brown. Line the bottom of a steamer with a few lettuce or cabbage leaves, then coat each slice of beef with ground rice and arrange in neat layers on top. Cover tightly.

3. Steam vigorously for 15 minutes. Garnish with sesame seed oil and more finely chopped spring onion. Serve hot. ·11·

Spring Rolls

Metric/Imperial
oil for deep-frying
Wrapping:
125 g/4 oz plain flour
250 ml/8 fl oz water
pinch of salt
Filling:
3 tablespoons oil
250 g/8 oz lean pork, shredded
125 g/4 oz celery, shredded
125 g/4 oz fresh mushrooms, shredded
1 tablespoon soy sauce
½ teaspoon salt
1 tablespoon cornflour, dissolved in 3 tablespoons water
Flour paste:
1 tablespoon plain flour mixed with 1 tablespoon water

1. To make the wrapping, sift the flour into a bowl and gradually beat in the water to form a smooth batter. Stir in the salt. Leave to stand for at least 30 minutes.

2. Lightly grease a heated 23 cm/9 inch frying pan. Use a pastry brush to spread a thin sheet of batter on the bottom of the pan. Cook until set. If holes appear, brush with a little more batter. Remove from

the pan and keep warm in a low oven. Continue making wrapping pancakes in this way until all of the batter is used.

3. For the filling, heat the oil in a wok. Add the pork and stir-fry until it changes colour. Add the vegetables, soy sauce and salt. Add the cornflour mixture and stir until thickened. Remove from the heat and allow to cool.

4. Place 2 tablespoons of the filling on the bottom half of each wrapping pancake and fold the top over. Fold the right side towards the left and the left side towards the right. Roll up into a tight roll and seal with the flour paste.

5. Heat the oil to 180°C/350°F. Deep-fry the rolls a few at a time until golden brown. Drain on absorbent kitchen paper and serve hot.

Spinach Salad

Metric/Imperial
750 g/1½ lb spinach
salt
freshly ground white pepper
2 tablespoons sesame seed oil
1 teaspoon sugar
1 teaspoon honey
2 tablespoons red wine vinegar
3 tablespoons soy sauce
1 teaspoon made mustard
1 slice root ginger, peeled and finely grated

1. Trim the spinach and wash thoroughly in cold water. Cook in a little boiling salted water until just tender. Drain well, then refresh under cold running water.

2. Squeeze out all the water from the spinach then tear each leaf into 3 or 4 pieces and place in a serving bowl. Allow to cool.

3. Combine the remaining ingredients and pour over the spinach. Toss well to completely coat the spinach with dressing. Serve well chilled.

Pork, Ham and Bamboo Shoot Soup

Metric/Imperial
50 g/2 oz pork fillet
2 teaspoons soy sauce
50 g/2 oz cooked ham
50 g/2 oz bamboo shoots
600 ml/1 pint clear stock (page 31)
1 teaspoon salt
1 teaspoon rice wine or dry sherry

1. Thinly slice the pork and mix it with the soy sauce.

2. Shred the ham and bamboo shoots.

3. Bring the stock to the boil, put in the pork, ham and bamboo shoots. When the soup starts to boil again, add the salt and wine or sherry and serve hot.

C · O · U · N · T · D · O · W · N

On the day:
Prepare the meats, vegetables, garnishes and Spring Rolls and refrigerate. Make the Spinach Salad.

To serve at 8.00 pm:
6.10: Prepare the meat and rice for the steamed beef.
6.45: Deep-fry the Spring Rolls. Fry the chicken and nuts and make the sauce.
7.15: Marinate the fish slices.
7.30: Boil the rice. Prepare the Steamed Beef.
7.45: Place the stock for the soup on to boil. Stir-fry and complete cooking the fish slices, and complete the Chicken with Cashew Nuts. Turn down the heat under the steamed beef and keep warm.
8.00: Finish the soup. Meanwhile fluff up the rice, transfer all the dishes to serving plates and serve.

Cook's Tip:
Chinese dried mushrooms are widely used for their aroma and flavour. Soak them in warm water for 20 to 30 minutes, then squeeze them dry and discard the hard stalks before use.

M·E·N·U

· 15 ·

A Memorable Meal for 4

Eight-Treasure Duck
Vegetables with Sweet and Sour Sauce
Steamed Chicken with Mushrooms

This dinner party menu is elaborate enough to satisfy the most adventurous gourmet, yet simple enough for even a novice to prepare. The centre-piece is a superb roast duck and the treasure in the title refers to the eight main ingredients in the stuffing.

Glutinous Rice
This rice is much favoured for stuffings. When cooked it becomes sticky and quite sweet and it is also extensively used for making cakes and sweetmeats. It may be black or white and is round-grained. Pudding rice can be used as a substitute but the texture will not be the same.

The Art of Steaming
Steamed Chicken with Mushrooms is a delicious dish. Ideally, you should use a Chinese bamboo steamer rather than a metal one. The bamboo lid is not absolutely airtight, so the steam dissipates rather than condenses on the inside of the lid. The Chinese often stack bamboo steamers on top of each other so that four or five dishes can be cooked simultaneously. Dishes that require more intense heat are put on the bottom layer, while delicate foods are placed furthest from the heat.

For a more formal occasion, simply add a delicious dessert such as, Date Crisps or Steamed Dumplings with Sweet Filling (see pages 12 and 24) and bring the meal to a traditional end by serving hot China tea.

Eight-Treasure Duck

Metric/Imperial

1 × 2 kg/4½-4¾ lb duckling
2 tablespoons dark soy sauce
Stuffing:
150 g/5 oz glutinous rice, cooked
200 ml/⅓ pint water
125 g/4 oz bamboo shoots
125 g/4 oz cooked ham
2 tablespoons oil
2 spring onions, finely chopped
2 slices root ginger, peeled and finely chopped
4-5 Chinese dried mushrooms, soaked in warm water for
*   20 minutes, squeezed dry, stemmed and chopped*
1 tablespoon dried shrimps, soaked in warm water for
*   20 minutes and drained*
½ teaspoon salt
1 tablespoon soy sauce
2 tablespoons rice wine or dry sherry
finely chopped spring onions, to garnish

1. Clean the duck well both inside and out, pat dry with paper towels, then brush the skin with the dark soy sauce. Cut the bamboo shoots and ham into small dice.
2. Heat the oil in a preheated wok, put in the spring onions and root ginger first, then add the mushrooms, ham, shrimps and bamboo shoots. Stir a few times, then add the salt, soy sauce and wine or sherry. Stir constantly until well blended, then turn off the heat, add the cooked rice and mix all the ingredients well to form the stuffing.
3. Pack the stuffing into the duck cavity and close up the tail opening. Place the duck on a wire tray on the top of a baking tin and put in a preheated oven (190°C/375°F), Gas Mark 5, for 30 minutes, then lower the oven temperature to (160°C/325°F), Gas Mark 3 for a further 45 minutes.
4. Either carve the duck at the table or cut it into small pieces and garnish with spring onions. ·13·

Vegetables with Sweet and Sour Sauce

Metric/Imperial

1 small red pepper, cored, seeded and cut into wedges
1 small green pepper, cored, seeded and cut into wedges
1 onion, cut into wedges
1 carrot, cut into wedges
2 celery sticks, sliced diagonally
1 tablespoon cornflour
1 tablespoon soy sauce
4 tablespoons demerara sugar
150 ml/¼ pint chicken stock
4 tablespoons vinegar
salt

1. Drop the vegetables into boiling water and simmer for 5 minutes. Mix the cornflour with the soy sauce until well blended.
2. Place the sugar, stock and vinegar in a saucepan, bring to the boil, then add the cornflour mixture. Simmer, stirring, for 2 to 3 minutes until thickened. Add the vegetables and season and reheat. ·2·

Steamed Chicken with Mushrooms

Metric/Imperial

750 g/1½-1¾ lb chicken meat
1 teaspoon salt
1 teaspoon sugar
1 tablespoon rice wine or dry sherry
1 teaspoon cornflour
3-4 Chinese dried mushrooms, soaked in warm water for
*   20 minutes, squeezed dry and stemmed*
2 slices root ginger, peeled
1 teaspoon oil
freshly ground Sichuan or black pepper
1 teaspoon sesame seed oil

Eight-treasure duck; Steamed chicken with mushrooms

1. Cut the chicken into bite-sized pieces and mix with the salt, sugar, wine or sherry and cornflour.
2. Thinly shred the mushrooms and root ginger. Grease a heatproof plate or dish with the oil.
3. Place the chicken pieces on the plate with the mushrooms and root ginger shreds on top, then add the ground pepper and sesame seed oil.
4. Place the chicken dish in a steamer and steam vigorously for 20 minutes. Serve hot. ·6·8·

Cook's Tip:
This dish is best using the breasts and thighs of a young chicken.

C · O · U · N · T · D · O · W · N

On the day:
Prepare the meats, vegetables and garnishes, cover and refrigerate. Soak and prepare the dried shrimps, and the mushrooms for the duck and chicken. Make the duck stuffing. Blanch the vegetables.

To serve at 8.00 pm:
6.15: Preheat the oven for the duck.
6.30: Start roasting the duck.
7.05: Reduce oven temperature as directed.
7.35: Steam the Chicken with Mushrooms.
7.45: Make the sweet and sour vegetables.
7.55: Finish the soup. Scrape the stuffing from the duck and place it in a serving bowl. Transfer all food to serving plates, garnish and serve immediately.

I · N · D · E · X

A · C · K · N · O · W · L · E · D · G · E · M · E · N · T · S

Bryce Attwell 22, 42, 58; Melvin Grey 7, 14, 19, 35, 50; Peter Myers 11, 27, 30, 38, 47, 55, 63.

Jacket photography: Clive Streeter   Illustration: Chloë Cheese
General Editor: Jenni Fleetwood   Art Editor: David Rowley   Production Controller: Sara Hunt